TEATIME
DISCIPLESHIP

FOR MOTHERS & DAUGHTERS

SALLY CLARKSON

HARVEST HOUSE PUBLISHERS
EUGENE, OREGON

To my children—
Sarah, Joy, and Keelia, Clay, Joel, Nathan,
you are my most delightful teatime companions.
Your lives have added so much beauty to mine, your words inspire,
your antics delight, your faith enlarges my own view of God.
Let's have a million more cups and transform our world together.

To my lovely granddaughters—
Lilian and Luci, I hope to share many inspiring
and delightful teatimes in our years together.

Special thanks to Keelia Clarkson, my beloved daughter-in-law,
for her excellent help in crafting some of our family stories
and traditions into life-giving words.

And to Jacqui, my dear tea angel.

By wisdom a house is built,
and through understanding it is established;
through knowledge its rooms are filled
with rare and beautiful treasures.

PROVERBS 24:3-4

CONTENTS

Tasting the Fruit of Discipleship {Intro}

Students are not greater than their teacher.
But the student who is fully trained will become like the teacher.

LUKE 6:40 NLT

Early one morning, I brewed my tea, lit a candle, turned on a favorite playlist, and sat to breathe in some peace before my day began. As usual, I had piles on my heart and mind and needed to center myself to prepare for a busy day. Before I work or settle in for a quiet moment with my tea, I turn off all digital notifications except those coming from my kids. So when I heard the ping announcing a new email, I opened it right away.

> *Dear Mama,*
>
> *I was thinking about you today. It seems every place I go, all the places I have lived, I hear your voice speaking to me. The hundreds of books we read out loud remind me of the heroines I want to become. The countless morning devotions speak to me through verses we discussed and memorized. The intimate talks on the front porch reserved just for me and you over a snack remind me that I am loved and cared for. Basically, you are a part of my being every day, and the messages you took time to share guide me wherever I go. I just didn't know if I had ever thanked you for taking the time. Mama, I appreciate all you did to shape great souls inside of us, and I love you so very much. That's all. Just wanted you to know.*
>
> *Love,*
> *A Clarkson child*

Of course, this note brought happy tears to my eyes and delighted my mother-heart. So often we sow into our children through love, teaching, serving, and giving our time endlessly, yet we aren't always sure if the seeds we planted are ever going to grow and bear fruit.

I read the note a second time, and a rush of memories flooded my mind—memories of the many women who showed me the value of discipleship and how to disciple other women and my children. This child of mine would not have had an example or experience for which to thank me had I not received those examples and experience in *my* journey.

That's why this book is in your hands. I want to continue the legacy by sharing with you how parenting discipleship unfolded in my life and providing simple and meaningful discipling moments for you to share with your daughter. If you know me at all, you will not be one bit surprised that I have chosen teatime as the backdrop for these special times. Life is just sweeter when a hot pot of tea and a lovely talk of faith are shared between two hearts. Though I wrote this book with mothers and daughters in mind, I have mentored my wonderful boys similarly—time stolen to be alone with tea and treats and talks. We followed the example of Tolkien and Lewis. So know that teatime is a great place to shape the hearts of our beloved boys as well.

Modeling our faith becomes mentoring a heart when we consistently pour into our child by talking openly, listening intently, praying together, and steeping in Scripture side by side. Whether you've been discipling others for years or this is your invitation to serve God in this way, you'll find there is nothing more meaningful or fruitful than discipling your kids and seeing what God does when your story and your child's story are explored in God's big, beautiful story.

How joyful are those who fear the LORD—all who follow his ways!
You will enjoy the fruit of your labor...
Your children will be like vigorous young olive trees
as they sit around your table.
That is the LORD's blessing for those who fear him.

Psalm 128:1-4 NLT

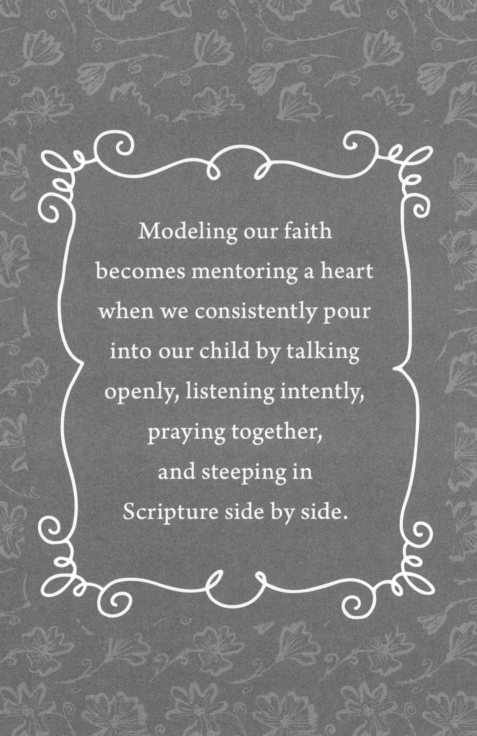

Modeling our faith
becomes mentoring a heart
when we consistently pour
into our child by talking
openly, listening intently,
praying together,
and steeping in
Scripture side by side.

When God Calls You

My sheep listen to my voice;
I know them, and they follow me.

JOHN 10:27

Bone-chilling fog wafted through the mysterious, ancient cobblestone streets as I made my way to school each morning in Kraków, Poland. Mists wrapped around the gray stone walls of the aged city, whispering of the hidden secrets of kings and queens who resided there through hundreds of years.

Living there during the Communist occupation meant we could not buy much food. Meat was scarce, and fresh fruit and vegetables were rare and brought into small, open-air markets only in season. But always we could find beautifully carved wooden boxes of every size, shape, and style.

Hoping that someday I would have my own cottage to fill with beauty and color, I would scan the hundreds of choices to find a distinctly crafted box that might someday find a place in my imagined future home. I was particularly drawn to the treasure chests that had keys to lock away precious letters, secrets, journals, or jewels.

Years later, when my home became a reality and little feet pattered around, my treasure chests became favorite relics in my home. Often, I would hide a verse scribbled on a piece of colored paper, some gold-covered chocolate coins, a tiny ring or bracelet, a knight in shining armor, or a small puzzle inside these boxes for my children to discover. Glee and intrigue would fill their hopeful little eyes as they opened the chest to see what was inside.

During a quiet time one morning, my eyes lighted upon one of my little chests, and the Holy Spirit impressed me to look at the hearts of my children as treasure chests. Filling their hearts with truth, beauty, love, great thoughts, books, ideas, adventures, memories, traditions, wisdom, music, art, lessons, and all the good things I could imagine became a purposeful goal. I wanted to fill them with such an abundance of relics of eternal value that they would draw beauty, strength, guidance, assurance, courage, and love from those deposits for the rest of their lives. God was clearly calling me to disciple my children. And just as my digital settings make sure I always hear messages from my kids, my spiritual settings make sure I always hear and answer a call from God. I was excited and committed.

I realized, though, that I could not give to them what I did not myself possess. If I wanted the souls of my children to be rich, then my soul needed to be rich because it was my soul they would draw from. And so the idea of intentionality began to engage the imagination of my heart. Whatever I filled my mind with, whatever I learned and embraced, flowed into the well of knowledge and refreshment I would draw from and pass on to them daily as I lived my moments in their presence. For example, investing time every morning with the Lord was of utmost importance because what I learned in those moments shaped the passion I passed to my family each morning over breakfast.

First, There Is a Foundation

I have been blessed by excellent women sprinkled along my life path who have invested deeply in my emotional and spiritual health. I never could have written books, had a national and local ministry, finished the course as an intentional mother in my home, and stayed faithful to my marriage without the help, support, comfort, and strength I received from other women. Differing in age, personality, educational background, and life experience, they each added a grace to the treasure chest of wisdom stowed inside my heart. Each has helped me to flourish when otherwise I would have floundered.

I began to grow from and appreciate this kind of intentional mentoring as a young woman, and even more so as I started a family. Discipling became a poignant focus of relationship I wanted to pass on to all my children. That day when I envisioned each of my children as a treasure chest to fill with the treasures of God's truth and the gems of God's grace, I became excited about parenting in a new way. Influence is best cultivated through love and friendship, so I prayed to deepen my sympathy for what was going on in their hearts at different ages, to understand their personalities, to affirm their intrinsic worth to me and to God and to others, and to encourage them daily.

My pursuit as a mother and discipler was to become the most mature and wise women I could be in my own life, and then, from that place, be an excellent woman reflecting my love for God. I knew it would be challenging for my daughters to find women with biblical ideals, so I wanted to be this example in front of my girls. I'm sure you carry the same concern and desire for your daughter. In response to this burden on my heart, I sought to grow in integrity and graciousness so my girls would have a model for the rest of their lives.

I'll admit that my imperfection and immaturity were evident along the journey, yet I gave all my heart and faith and effort to the hands of Jesus and kept going one day after another toward my goals. This, dear mom, is what you can do too. You don't need a teaching degree. You don't need a master of divinity. You don't need a ribbon of honor for oratory achievements. All you need as your foundation to begin is a heart for Jesus and for your child—that is how you answer the call to discipleship.

A Legacy of Love

When we set in motion traditions formed by faith and values in action, a legacy of love that begins with Jesus is strengthened in our homes. The day our children notice that we aren't just praying at the dinner table, but in every circumstance, is a moment they tuck away as a guide to and evidence of living a faithful life. Later, when times become difficult for the growing child or when tensions rise at home, those memories remain, and the lessons experienced through intentional discipling and from our example of living a sincere faith are there as a foundation.

Don't ever believe your child isn't noticing how you live and how you interact with them as well as others. They see it all. They make note of our priorities and how we invest our time and resources. And when they realize they are one of those top priorities and you are choosing to pour into them with time, prayer, teaching, and connection, they get a glimpse of God's love and care for them. Parenting through the lens of mentoring and discipleship will inspire, train, and stretch us and our children to live into our God-given potential.

When we are given the gift to add to and continue a legacy of God's love shared between women and between generations, we are transformed. I am a different person because of the faithfulness, encouragement, and inspiration I gave to and received from my friends, and now my daughters.

I remember your genuine faith, for you share the
faith that first filled your grandmother Lois and your mother,
Eunice. And I know that same faith continues strong in you.

2 Timothy 1:5 NLT

For Such a Time as This

Why is it more important than ever to be accountable to our girls? To give them an identity as beautiful women who can think, create, and love as they nurture education, family, and marriage in their homes? It is because the belief in the fulness of biblical femininity has been lost in a sea of the extremes of femininity that are put forth.

In this time in history, there is more competition than ever for the soul and brain space of all of us. With smartphones and social media, we are bombarded with messages from a secular culture that challenge our biblical convictions and teach a contrasting morality, a relative set of values. Add to that, the church seems to be filled with leaders and believers who have diminished their stories with compromises of every kind.

Who knows but that you have come to
your royal position for such a time as this?

Esther 4:14

This meaningful
endeavor is for such
a time as this in your
story too. By answering
God's call to discipleship,
you and your daughter
will forever be changed.

It is more important than ever for our children to deeply feel our love and experience great joy and friendship with us so they will continue wanting our input and influence in their lives. Parents are created by God to come alongside to champion, help, and encourage their children to live into their God-designed destinies.

Every step toward deepening your relationship with your daughter and her relationship with the Lord is needed for such a time as this—not only in terms of history, but for this season in your daughter's life. And I imagine this meaningful endeavor is for such a time as this in your story too. By answering God's call to discipleship, you and your daughter will forever be changed.

Expressing your love for your daughter and the condition of her heart will do much to encourage her. And sharing these times over tea adds a ritual of sweet connection that won't be lost if things aren't perfect. You should know up front that things won't be perfect. And they will be lovely and rewarding just the same. Even *that* is a life and faith lesson for your young daughter.

The most significant influence comes through an atmosphere of unconditional love, through pleasant experiences shared, through trust and conversations. It's because of the commitments we cultivate over time and the willingness to be vulnerable and authentic that we bring about support and encouragement, communication and connection, respect and understanding—all the blessings true friendships have in common.

Your desire for a deeper friendship with your daughter will be evident in your commitment to spend time with her when the focus isn't on homework or household chores or negotiating technology time. Speaking of which, let's not forget that we are the most connected generation technologically and the most isolated from our neighbors. It requires more effort and forethought—and sometimes plain courage and boldness—to reach out to others in person. Women in this era have either forgotten the intrinsic potential they have as women sharing in friendship, faith, and community, or they are too distracted, overwhelmed, and busy to access the glory and beauty of their femininity and how it blooms more fully in the context of loving relationships. Many are afraid or reticent to embrace the delight and joy of discipleship as a regular and valued part of their experiences.

I think one reason there is hesitation is because we don't experience this fellowship cultivated the way some have in past decades. We need only to look back a generation to be reminded that companionship, deep connection, and kinship among women has been a rich reality throughout all cultures and centuries. No matter the challenging and complicated historical chapters of life they have found themselves in, women appreciated their God-given heritage and story. They understood the legacy of love, wisdom, and skill they could live into by seeing it played out before them organically, day in and day out, with neighbors and relatives—a community of women who lived close by.

Restoring Heart-to-Heart Connection

Discipleship on the home front will help to restore the rhythm and ritual of connecting heart-to-heart. As you model the cultivation of female friendships that provide emotional affirmation and faith encouragement, may your heart's imagination be captivated by the impact you will have on your daughter. What you share now in these intentional times stays with your daughter as she matures, makes tough decisions, moves away, has other mentors, creates her own circle of friends, and becomes a life-giver for others. You will help her today *and* also build up her amazing story to be lived as a woman made in God's image to share His light with the world.

When I embraced the call, I knew I needed to make plans or the busyness of life would take over my good intentions. I started with too many objectives, making mentoring far harder than it needed to be. But over time I narrowed down my goals. I decided I wanted to gather verses of God's truth and wisdom to place inside their hearts so they could draw from them all their days no matter where life and God took them. I also knew I wanted a simple way to draw them close and to make our shared talks personal, beautiful, and impactful.

This is why I cultivated a teatime discipleship experience as a foundation. I met with my children individually over tea and over many years to invest these treasures in their hearts. These intimate friendship times were the space where I was able to build in them a sense of the truths that they could build their lives around.

Truth, beauty, and wisdom must be intentionally passed down. Rich souls do not exist by accident. Pouring into your child requires a commitment to what you most want your daughter to hide inside her heart and soul and how you can encourage that to happen. If you pause with concern you won't do this right, let me assure you that you *will* do it right because you're embarking on a new journey with a desire to show your daughter the love of Jesus. Perfection is not a requirement. I wouldn't be able to speak to this if not for my own daughters and how they received this one-on-one mentoring even when I stumbled. And my girls eventually made discipleship with other women, friends, communities, and their own families a pursuit and passion. It's a sight that brings joy to a mother's heart.

There are many treasures to be found and shared and shared again as you and your daughter become a part of this legacy circle of fellowship and discipleship between women. It will change your relationship, outlook, understanding of God, and your purpose. And, I do believe, it will change the world.

Come along inside…
We'll see if tea and buns can make the world a better place.
Kenneth Grahame, *The Wind in the Willows*

INTENTIONAL COMMITMENTS

One quiet morning, I journaled five commitments I would make to become a loving, effective discipler to my children and pour into them the riches of great stories, Scripture's wisdom, and life-giving words.

I will welcome my children to come to me anytime as a trusted friend, mentor, and helper. I will say yes to their desire to talk even when inconvenient. I'll avoid frustration by laying aside expectations to control life and commit to showing the love of Jesus.

I will create a safe place where they can say anything, ask any question, and know I will keep their confidences, hold their trust, and understand their failures. I want to be someone they count on.

I will prepare ahead for each discipleship time. I understand I cannot pass on what I have not first personally invested in. I will study my Bible so my children will draw out of my heart the faith riches I store there.

I will be a conductor of life-giving moments of beauty, feasting, and living companionship. With candles, music, and treats, I will nurture an atmosphere of pleasure, fun, rest, and celebration to create growth.

I will focus on my hope for my children that they will receive a legacy of God's Word, wisdom for life, and training in character. I want them to leave home with foundations of biblical truth and virtue holding them and supporting them.

YOUR
COMMITMENTS

Spend time with a cup of tea and this planning page. Prayerfully complete the five commitments.

How I will strive to be an available presence to my
child even when it's inconvenient...

How I will become a safe, supportive discipler and
establish trust with my daughter...

How I will prepare for discipleship times and deepen
my faith to better share God's love...

Ways I might cultivate creativity, beauty, treats,
and joy for our times together...

What is my great hope for her and her future? How I will
focus on what I pour into my daughter's heart...

Tea for Two

A joy shared is a joy doubled.

JOHANN WOLFGANG VON GOETHE

An unfamiliar darkness hovered in my daughter's deep, beautiful eyes. Life's small issues had piled high on her heart and had drained the smile from her face. Her brows furrowed, and she decided an escape to her room to pour out her thoughts in a journal was the best solution.

While she was tucked away brooding and getting her emotions out onto the page, I pondered how to help lift the burden off her shoulders a wee bit. I wanted to make things better, easier, lighter in some way. Isn't that the triage response of every mom? We can't always fix a situation, nor should we consider ourselves to be the one in charge of fixing; however, we are fortunate to be the ones who are in the perfect position to come alongside our daughter and guide her in God's truth and love. We can invite her to a way of thinking and believing that shifts her toward a healthier place mentally, emotionally, physically, and spiritually.

A Personal Invitation

An idea burst into my brain space and got me motivated. Quickly, I moved my old wheel-adorned tea cart between two overstuffed chairs by the window that looked out at shimmering aspen trees. Next, to make this scene special, I set the little cart with some of my mother's favorite dishes that she had passed down to me. They are gold-rimmed beauties that look and feel elegant—sure to elevate any get-together. Especially one created in a matter of minutes! Then I carefully selected and placed two of our favorite teacups along with silverware and linen napkins. For a glimmer of light to represent the glimmer of hope I had for my daughter's heart, I placed a votive candle

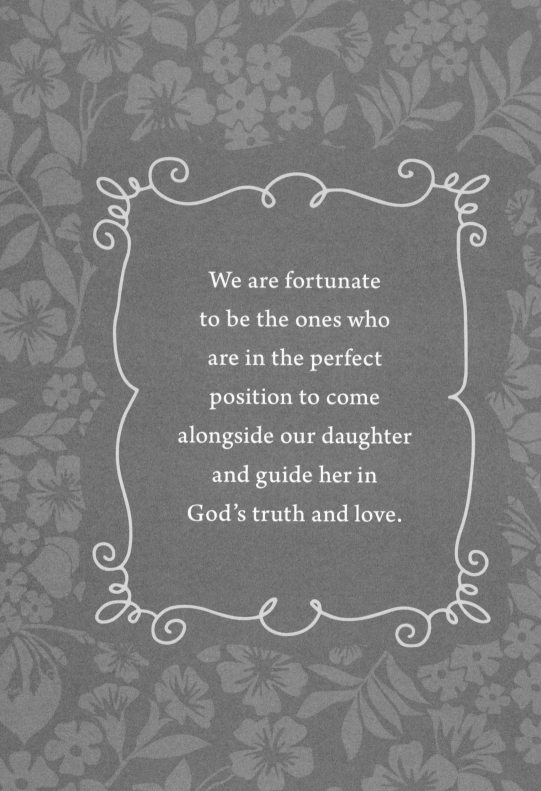

We are fortunate
to be the ones who
are in the perfect
position to come
alongside our daughter
and guide her in
God's truth and love.

on each side of both our plates. Finally, I created an impromptu centerpiece with wild-flowers plucked from my yard and placed in a sweet little vase.

I paused to consider how to add more sensory delights to the table. After a quick inventory of the kitchen cupboards, I reached for homemade bread and sliced and toasted two big pieces and then slathered them with butter. What is better than butter? Not much. However, a pot of raspberry jam is always a lovely complement. Next, I put together a variety of tastes: slices of cheese and deli turkey rolled into logs; a cluster of salted buttered pecans; a small pile of ruby red raspberries (my daughter's favorite); a handful of chocolate almonds; and a chocolate chip cookie. Snack meals, as we called these types of meals, had delighted my daughter since she was a little girl. I knew this selection would bring a smile.

Finally, and in my opinion most importantly, I prepared the tea with steaming hot water and three tea bags. I set the worn, loved pot on the table, grabbed a sugar bowl and tiny pitcher of milk, and within 15 minutes I had created a space for encourage-ment, friendship, and love.

Folding a 3 x 5 card in half, I penned a short note and set it by her plate.

Precious one, I am sorry for the sadness you are carrying. You are so very special to me, and I love you to the moon. Shall we be friends and take a few moments to share our hearts? Praying for you.

All my love, Mama

I climbed the stairs to my daughter's room and softly knocked on the door. "Come in," she murmured.

I poked my head around the edge of the door. "I created a little cheer-you-up party because I know you could use some encouragement. Will you join me downstairs?"

She looked up from her journal and gave the invite some consideration. Apparently, the offer of a party for two appealed to her. She stood up and followed me down the stairs where the candles shimmered, the music from my small speaker filled the room, and those simple extra touches were displayed.

I knew it was a success when she gave a soft squeal. "Oh, Mama! This is just what I needed. It's beautiful."

And so we made one more memory, dug deeper the pathways of our friendship, and found just the encouragement she needed. And might I add, this time together encouraged my own heart in ways I hadn't realized I needed.

Tea for two, and two for tea,
Me for you, and you for me
Irving Caesar, "Tea for Two"

The Shared Joy of Discipleship

This is just a small picture of what I hope will inspire you in this book. As a woman, perhaps as a friend or mom, you have a unique capacity to pass on words of faith, to help spiritually form another person, to provide an example that another will carry into their lives wherever they go. It will become their own as they partner with God for next steps, a vision and hope for their futures, and a sense of their part in God's story.

All of us long for a companion to share in our hopes, burdens, and dreams. We were made for friendship. But I believe God especially crafted women with a deep desire to be known and deeply beloved in friendship as well as with a capacity to civilize life, to create beauty, and to give words of hope and faith. Doing this with our own families is one of the great treasures and joys we are given.

Teatime discipleship is a legacy I have left in the hearts, minds, and souls of my own daughters and sons, celebrating life together hundreds of times in this way. When asked why all four of my children believe deeply in God, all of them almost always say, "It was the great food, the feasting together through life, the encouragement given, the emphasis on beauty and conversation, the faith that was passed on through so many intentional times together."

I have lived through the young restlessness and foolish ideas of girlhood, the hormones and emotions and frustration of preteens, the "I am an adult, and I think I know what is best in life" teen years, and even young adulthood! Yet, as together we marveled at the scope of God's goodness over a steaming cup of tea and a delectable treat, it quickened us together to hope, to imagine, to dream of what might just be possible. In those sweet pauses of sipping tea and listening to one another, we also discovered a deepening sense of purpose and a clearer picture of our stories within God's greater story.

I would sprinkle in questions:

What is on your heart today?

What do you hope for?

What are your dreams?

What do you think God is calling you to become?

Those questions and the shared moments in which we held up these thoughts to God's light are deeply formative, marked by a shared commitment to the open horizons of possibility made real by faith. I often felt these teatimes were our way of reaching toward the ideals that most drove us   the dreams of study, artistry, travel, or ministry that filled our hearts. Many of the dreams my girls have spent years pursuing and attaining—PhDs, writing books, education at Oxford, marriage, creating loving homes, teaching—were first expressed as whispered wishes and prayed-for hopes in those lovely teatime hours.

Companionship of soul and mind requires planning, purpose, and choice. Those treasured shared spaces in so many of our homes and shared moments and the community of family and friends that grew from them didn't happen on their own. They were crafted, sought, chosen, and claimed times, times when we said no to other commitments or work.

I realize those intentional teatimes taught me, as a mom, something else as well: Deep, long-term, soul-satisfying discipleship takes hard work and heart work.

I chose to intentionally spend time beyond the lure of my writing deadlines, work, or sleep, often sacrificing my personal time. All my children now prioritize times together and with dear local friends all over the world. When we are together, our conversations continue to be shaped by thoughtful questions purposefully asked, by our intent to know and be known. This is one of the threads that connects our hearts, convictions, values, and faith because these priorities were shaped over many years of intentionality.

Tea and Sympathy

Building a friendship with your daughter and establishing the privilege of having a mentoring influence on her life doesn't just happen. It is a gift, but it isn't one dropped into our laps to be received. I have come to understand that this discipleship connection with our children is something we craft and provide, a work and an art we make space for again and again, a priority we choose amid the demands of life. These meaningful relationships require concerted, often intensive effort.

What better way to suggest friendliness—
and to create it—than with a cup of tea?

J. Grayson Luttrell

In a world where so many feel alone, isolated, and misunderstood, we can come along beside our beloved ones and be a source of life, faith, and love to them. It is my hope that you will catch this vision in the pages of this book, and that you, too, will become an artist of beauty through your own life as a teatime discipler.

Each of us has a different personality, a unique story to live, and freedom to create these life-giving moments in our own way. More variety is sprinkled in as we also factor in the conversation topics or special touches that will mean the most to our guest—in this case, the ways we can add delight for our daughters. A teatime can be simple.

Often, when the kids were young, I fit these moments into small spaces of time between the normal events of my life and would reach for whatever was in the pantry

Long-term,
soul-satisfying
discipleship takes
hard work and
heart work.

and refrigerator. Other times, I planned and made a special event of our time together with delicious fare and personalized decorations.

But always there was (and is) a hot cup of tea at the heart of it—a sort of anchor to our times.

Yet most important was that I had developed an intention and rhythm for these special times to give words of love, to guide us toward shared wisdom, to inspire faith. Coming to each person, each child with a sympathetic heart that said, "I am listening. I want to know what is on your heart and understand your thoughts and dreams. You are precious to me, and I believe in the story God has created you to tell through the days of your life."

Hidden Treasures

When we memorize Scripture, when we think about it over a lifetime, it guides us into wise choices, trust in God, and eternal hope. It is a reservoir of comfort and guidance that no one can steal or destroy. The ever-filling, ever-full well of God's Word also protects us from falling short of—or missing altogether—the hope and purpose God has placed within us. Those life-giving words heal and lead us forward in our unique purpose and path.

I have hidden your word in my heart
that I might not sin against you.

Psalm 119:11

I believe our words, messages, and encouragements are hidden in the hearts of our children and guide them. Words have power. Sadly, so many of us know this because of negative or hurtful words we've received from others or even tell ourselves. They are hard to shake off, aren't they? In fact, they tend to be the words we believe most unless we have guarded our hearts with God's truths about us and about who He is. Our children need this protection desperately.

As you journey through this discipling adventure with your child, you will begin to notice the impact of good words, God-words, on both of your lives.

Stick with what you learned and believed, sure of the integrity of your teachers—why, you took in the sacred Scriptures with your mother's milk! There's nothing like the written Word of God for showing you the way to salvation through faith in Christ Jesus. Every part of Scripture is God-breathed and useful one way or another—showing us truth, exposing our rebellion, correcting our mistakes, training us to live God's way. Through the Word we are put together and shaped up for the tasks God has for us.

2 Timothy 3:14-17 MSG

Show your beloved child how taking in God-breathed words and nestling them in her heart will prepare her and embolden her for the story God has planned. Memorizing verses is not an act of rote obedience but a transformative act of nourishment, love, and strength for our journeys of purpose and faith.

This knowledge and truth will hold her fast in her years as an adult because the deepest places have been formed by intentional times, conversations, and training that took place in the years with you as her guide and mentor.

A Heart Expressed

Feasting on God's Word fills us. His truths become a part of our makeup and transforms our spiritual DNA. Walking forward with a changed mind and spirit turns our hearts to God and to the rich relationship we can have with our Creator. Prayer is our way to express our hearts when they overflow with gratitude and praise, ache from struggle, or cry out for help.

Show your beloved
child how taking in
God-breathed
words and nestling
them in her heart
will prepare her and
embolden her for the
story God has planned.

One day Jesus was praying in a certain place.
When he finished, one of his disciples said to him,
"Lord, teach us to pray, just as John taught his disciples."

Luke 11:1

Jesus showed the disciples how to pray, and He shared what we call the Lord's Prayer. It is a beautiful example of how to come to the Lord with our hopes, fears, and praise. You are carrying on this legacy each time you pray with, for, and over your daughter. She will be attuned to the ways of prayer because your invitations to prayer time will show her how natural it is to reach out to God for everything. "Rejoice always, pray continually, give thanks in all circumstances; for this is God's will for you in Christ Jesus" (1 Thessalonians 5:16-18). When a heart is softened for prayer and open to God's voice, this idea of praying continually or without ceasing goes from being an assumed exaggerated premise to an actual faith practice: a lifeline to God for our children.

We greatly bless our kids when we dispel the false belief that prayer is rigid or requires saying all the right words and in the just-right righteous tone. Through a discipling relationship we can replace misconceptions with a vision of a continuous connection between Jesus and them. In the times of tea and discipleship—as well as in everyday life—your modeling of the ease and possibility of prayer will free your precious one to express her heart sincerely, humbly, and personally to the Lord. Is there any greater heirloom of faith to share?

Mentoring and Making Memories

Each of the six teatimes in this book present a picture of what I did to pour into the lives of my children intentionally. I would make some wonderful treat, light candles, put on beautiful music, and then have a discipleship teatime with them. We would read a story together, memorize the character quality, and then read and discuss together the application of why these virtues were treasures to keep forever and how they could be applied to life. In this way, I prepared my children to go confidently into their secular worlds with foundations of truth and wisdom that would hold them through the seasons of their lives.

Each tea has the same structure, so as you move through the discipling times, you will become more comfortable with the flow, as will your daughter. Here is a glimpse of what you will experience together in each of the following teatime discipleship chapters:

Intro—A sharing from my life to start you off. I encourage you to read this to your daughter.

Steep in Scripture Together—A Bible story about a woman of Scripture and her godly character, to be read aloud together or you can take turns reading these offerings throughout.

Conversation and Connection—Record and discuss wisdom from the Bible story.

Passages to Ponder—Read and discuss select Scriptures with guided questions. Depending on your daughter's preferences and the amount of time you have, you may suggest journaling answers in a separate book and then sharing from those responses.

Pour into Your Girl's Heart—Fill the cup of your daughter's faith and character by sharing aloud what you witness in her life and by reading verses personalized to speak directly to her heart.

Mother's Prayer—Personalize and read this prayer aloud to bless your daughter.

Daughter's Prayer—Invite your daughter to read this prayer aloud. These prayers will shape her comfort and confidence in praying. And should she want to continue in her own words—all the better!

Two for Tea—Ideas, recipes, and a "Make It Special" section with suggestions when you have more time to personalize or deepen the discipling time.

I picture you taking time with your daughter and giving her treasures that will last a lifetime and beyond. May you make sweet memories, and may you be richly blessed in your time together.

3

PURPOSE
AND
CONFIDENCE

Purpose

Something set up as an object or end to be attained.

Confidence

The quality or state of being certain.

May God our Father himself and our Master Jesus clear the road to you!
And may the Master pour on the love so it fills your lives
and splashes over on everyone around you, just as it does from us to you.
May you be infused with strength and purity,
filled with confidence in the presence of God our Father
when our Master Jesus arrives with all his followers.

1 THESSALONIANS 3:11-13 MSG

"I know the plans I have for you," declares the Lord,
"plans to prosper you and not to harm you,
plans to give you hope and a future."
Jeremiah 29:11

In my younger years, as a new Christian with a deep desire to help lead others to Christ, I worked as a missionary behind the Iron Curtain in Eastern Europe. I smuggled in biblical literature and spent my days bringing the good news of the gospel to those I came across, introducing them to their Creator.

During this time, this formative, exciting, unpredictable time, I began to realize that my life was a story I was telling—much like any of the fantastical tales, the romantic movies, or the heart-touching novels I loved. I watched as God worked through me to build His kingdom on earth, and in doing so I discovered that I could play a meaningful role in His eternal story.

It was these unforgettable years in Eastern Europe and the awareness of the story I was living out that led us to start a Clarkson tradition. When each of our children turned 15, starting with Sarah, my oldest, I would take them to my old stomping grounds—all the way across the vast, sparkling Atlantic Ocean from our sweet, familiar home in Colorado to Europe, the very place where I'd first understood that I could live into a bigger story.

Every chapter of our adventure, from stuffing ourselves into an overcrowded plane to landing in an entirely different country and wandering along the cobblestone streets, served as a reminder that there was a massive, beautiful world to live in and a significant story being told—and as part of God's creation, they could be a part of it.

With every new path we forged and every old haunt of mine we visited, I saw it dawn on my children how meaningful the story was *they* were telling with their lives. I saw them yearning to take ownership of their story—to write it, to tell it, to love it, and to walk confidently in it. It was profoundly important for my children, especially as they began their journey into adulthood—just as it was for me—to recognize the part we each have to play in God's story. This was something I longed for my children to understand—that they are a treasure in His eyes, they are the art of His creative hand, and they have a purpose to live out. Simply put, this is the influence and importance of parenting.

Some might say motherhood is your biblical duty and end the conversation there. But I've been blessed to discover the greatest purpose and joy in this calling of motherhood: It is a ministry. It is discipleship.

Before He departed to be with the Father, Jesus gave us one great command: "Make disciples!" (Matthew 28:19). We're charged with making followers of Jesus. If we look further back in God's Word, we realize the mission began at the beginning. In the book of Genesis, when the world is being formed by the Creator's hands and before Adam and Eve fell into sin, God looked upon these two and gave them the mandate to "fill the earth" (Genesis 1:28). The implicit hope in that phrase is the belief that those who filled the earth would follow the Creator.

But then there was the fall. The birth of sin disrupted the birth of the vision behind this mandate. You and I and our daughters now live in a broken world. God's design and plan for family has been distorted, but it has not changed.

These mother-and-daughter discipleship teatimes will pour the beauty of God's design and purpose into your hearts. These moments and the longer journey are shaping and influencing your stories as mother and child, as individual women of God, and as daughters of the Father. When you and I share from our early stories, we give our children a glimpse of what it looks like to walk with God at every age and through every circumstance.

Our story in God emboldens us to pursue the dreams He's placed on our hearts and to use our gifts to serve Him, our families, and the people God brings into our lives. "God doesn't want us to be shy with his gifts, but bold and loving and sensible" (2 Timothy 1:7 MSG).

My children's understanding of the unique role they were created to play in His great story will guide them for the rest of their lives, informing their every decision as well as how they see themselves and how they relate to those around them. Even in difficult, trying times, being aware of their role in God's kingdom continues to give them the perception that their choices, their days, and their lives have eternal effects and lasting meaning.

Let's immerse ourselves in God's Word and conversation about purpose and confidence.

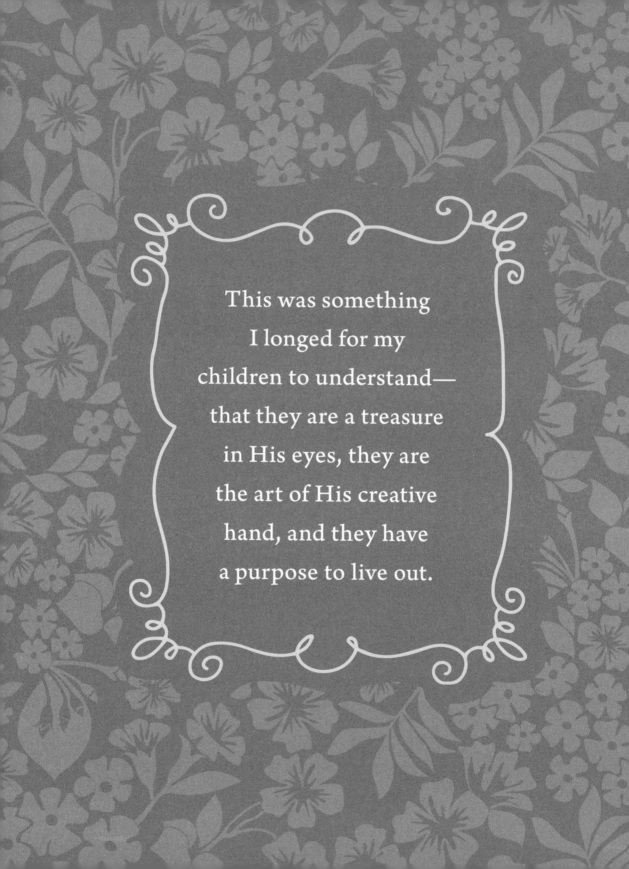

This was something
I longed for my
children to understand—
that they are a treasure
in His eyes, they are
the art of His creative
hand, and they have
a purpose to live out.

STEEP IN
SCRIPTURE TOGETHER

Scripture is full of stories illustrating the significance of owning the story we're telling with our lives, and one of my personal favorites is that of Rahab.

When we meet Rahab in Scripture, her story is wrought with brokenness, hardship, and misfortune. Despite everything she had going against her, she took hold of the story God had for her to tell, and she became a heroine of the Bible in the process.

When two Israelite spies came to her city of Jericho, Rahab knew there would be an attack on the city soon. She also knew the Israelites were God's chosen people and decided to help them, asking that she and her family be spared in exchange for offering them a place to hide:

Before the spies were down for the night, the woman came up to them
on the roof and said, "I know that God has given you the land. We're all afraid.
Everyone in the country feels hopeless. We heard how GOD dried
up the waters of the Red Sea before you when you left Egypt, and what he did
to the two Amorite kings east of the Jordan, Sihon and Og, whom you put
under a holy curse and destroyed. We heard it and our hearts sank. We all had
the wind knocked out of us. And all because of you, you and God, your God,
God of the heavens above and God of the earth below.

"Now promise me by GOD. I showed you mercy; now show my
family mercy. And give me some tangible proof, a guarantee of life
for my father and mother, my brothers and sisters—everyone
connected with my family. Save our souls from death!"

Joshua 2:8-13 MSG

The men agreed, and Rahab was able to take charge of the story God had for her and save her family. Rahab's confidence came from her faith and allowed her to step forward with courage to be a part of God's plan. And all along, God had chosen Rahab to be a big part of His story. When Jericho fell, Rahab and her family were kept safe because of Rahab's faith that she had a part to play by taking initiative to talk boldly to the spies and living out God's story for her—which included being a part of Jesus's ancestral line. Just think, this woman with little value or power in the world was highly valued by God. Because she was willing to follow God's calling on her life, she walked in confidence of being known and used by God for His good purposes. She accepted the challenge while she still had fear. But bigger than that fear was her trust in God's faithfulness.

We are given these opportunities too. When we are called to act, to speak, or to show up bravely as the person God made us to be, we can trust Him to be faithful. We don't need the power, wealth, or acceptance of people around us. We only need the power of God's purpose and a heart of obedience to change the world.

Write your answers below and then take a moment to share them with one another.

When have you, like Rahab, acted in confidence because of your faith in God?
What happened?

MOTHER

DAUGHTER

If in doubt MAKE tea

PASSAGES TO PONDER

You are deeply loved by God. You were uniquely crafted by Him, and He has a story for you to tell with your life. We find evidence of this throughout Scripture. These are some verses I look to when encouraging my daughters to live their story of purpose.

> **We are God's handiwork, created in Christ Jesus to do good works, which God prepared in advance for us to do.**
> **Ephesians 2:10**

1. How does it feel to know that God created you uniquely?
2. What good works is He leading you to do right now?

> **He who began a good work in you will carry it on to completion until the day of Christ Jesus.**
> **Philippians 1:6**

1. Does it comfort you to know that God will complete His good work in you?
2. Where do you place your confidence, and how does your confidence show?

> **The LORD your God is with you, the Mighty Warrior who saves. He will take great delight in you; in his love he will no longer rebuke you, but will rejoice over you with singing.**
> **Zephaniah 3:17**

1. Do you believe God is with you?
2. Why do you think God takes great delight in us?

POUR INTO YOUR GIRL'S HEART

(Use your daughter's name for each of the blanks.)

Dear _____

You have been called by God for a purpose. When you walk in faith, side by side with the Lord, you'll be able to hear His leading, His encouragement, and His guidance. It's exciting to be your mom and witness God at work in your life.

   I want to pour a sense of purpose into your heart. I pray you will take hold of God's truth along your path of becoming who you are and confidently living the story God has for you. These are the ways I am seeing purpose and confidence in your life.

Take in God's Word as I read these verses personalized just for you:

We know that in all things God works for the good of _____,
who loves him, who has been called according to his purpose.
Based on Romans 8:28

_____, be generous with the different things God gave you,
passing them around so all get in on it:
If words, let it be God's words;
if help, let it be God's hearty help.
Based on 1 Peter 4:10-11

Long before we first heard of Christ and got our hopes up,
he had his eye on _____, had designs on _____
for glorious living, part of the overall purpose he is
working out in everything and everyone.
Based on Ephesians 1:11-12 MSG

MOTHER'S PRAYER

(Use your daughter's name)

Jesus,

May Your Word take root in _____'s spirit as she grows

and discovers who You are and how she is Your beloved daughter.

Help me to remind her of her value as one of God's children.

When _____ is struggling to hear Your voice or know Your way, let her

return to Your Word and to the truths we learn in our times of discipleship.

Fill her heart with certainty that You are with her

and You are shaping her days with Your loving hands.

Thank You for allowing me to be her mom

and for our times exploring our faith and trust in You.

Being a part of Your story, my story,

and _____'s story is my greatest joy.

In Jesus's name, amen.

DAUGHTER'S PRAYER

Dear Jesus,

Thank You for loving me and for creating me for a purpose.

I'm excited to learn more about my unique story as a part of Your bigger story.

Show me the way I should go, Lord.

Prepare my heart and give me a spirit of confidence so I can walk in

faith toward all You invite me to know and do.

In hard times, remind me how special I am to You

and that You will never leave me.

I trust Your promise that in You alone I will discover who I am and my purpose.

In Jesus's name, amen.

TWO FOR TEA

Cambric tea was hot water and milk, with only a taste of tea in it,
but little girls felt grown-up when their mothers let them drink cambric tea.

LAURA INGALLS WILDER, *THE LONG WINTER*

When mothers and children pause to take a break together and with the Lord, they create a meaningful ritual. I'm happy to share from this point in my life as a mom to grown children that my many years of inviting each child for a time of connection and conversation over tea has made a lasting impression on their faiths and lives. It has also created in them a longing for moments of stillness and calm so they can listen to their hearts and to God's heart for them. And now I get the great honor of sharing this with grandchildren…and with you and your children.

Feel free to prepare whatever kind of tea you would like. For inspiration, our quote today from *The Long Winter* serves up a great idea as a beginner tea for young girls. Some make cambric tea without any tea at all as a soothing substitute, but you can guess my advice—bring on the tea! What a treat to introduce your daughter to the wonders of a classic beverage and the practice of fellowshipping while sipping.

◆━━◆━◆━━◆

CAMBRIC TEA

Place 1 to 2 teaspoons of sugar in a pretty teacup

Add ⅓ cup of cold milk—let the sugar dissolve

Pour ⅓ cup boiling water

Pour ⅓ cup brewed black tea (my favorite is Yorkshire Gold)

Add a drop of vanilla if desired

Make It Special

You can go all out or keep everything simple. Remember my
story of crafting an impromptu invitation for my daughter
with a folded 3 x 5 card? It doesn't get simpler than that.
When your heart is in it, easy is just as meaningful.

⬥—◀▮▶—⬥

For your first teatime, consider buying a pretty teacup
for your daughter. Or build anticipation for these times together and take your
daughter shopping in advance to choose
her own teacup. Many antique stores sell beautiful, inexpensive cups that have
been orphaned from their sets.

⬥—◀▮▶—⬥

Place a small bouquet of flowers from your garden or the supermarket as a
centerpiece. Consider your daughter's favorite colors. Appreciating beauty
together will be a lasting memory.

⬥—◀▮▶—⬥

Serve water in a clear pitcher with lemon slices. This complements the
Lemon Blueberry Drizzle Loaf if you choose it for your tea, and it's a pretty
presentation even if you don't.

⬥—◀▮▶—⬥

Everything has a story…even our teacups! If you have
a family tea set or you chose a special cup for your
daughter, share its story if you'd like.

TEATIME TREATS

Teatime feasts were always highly anticipated in the Clarkson household. We all looked forward to gathering and celebrating over something filling, joyful, and delicious—and what is more celebratory and light filled than a lemon blueberry drizzle loaf?

LEMON BLUEBERRY DRIZZLE LOAF

Ingredients for the loaf
1 cup unsalted butter (softened)
1 cup finely ground (caster) sugar
3 eggs
¾ tsp. lemon juice
3½ T. whole milk
1½ cups self-rising flour
¼ tsp. baking soda
Zest of 2 to 3 lemons
Pinch of salt
1 cup blueberries

Ingredients for the drizzle
½ cup finely ground (caster) sugar
2¼ T. lemon juice

Ingredients for the lemon icing (optional)
1 tsp. salted butter
⅓ cup lemon juice
1¾ cups powdered sugar

Preheat the oven to 350° F. Line a 2-pound loaf tin with parchment paper. With a hand-held or stand mixer, cream the butter and sugar until smooth and fluffy. In a separate medium bowl, whisk together the eggs, lemon juice, and milk until fully combined. Slowly beat in the egg mixture to the butter mixture, making sure to mix well. In another medium bowl, mix together the flour, baking soda, lemon zest, and salt. Fold the dry ingredients into the wet ingredients until just combined, adding in the blueberries after everything else is mixed in. Pour the batter into the loaf tin and bake for 50 to 60 minutes or until an inserted toothpick comes out clean.

While the loaf is baking, mix together the caster sugar and the lemon juice to make the drizzle. Once the loaf is done baking and while it's still hot, poke small holes along the top with a toothpick so the drizzle will seep in. Then pour the lemon drizzle over the top of the loaf. Leave the loaf in the tin for a few minutes before transferring it to a cooling rack.

While the loaf cools, beat together the butter and lemon juice for the icing. Gradually add in the powdered sugar, working out the lumps, and mix until smooth. Once the loaf has cooled, take a spoon and drizzle the icing along the top in a zigzag formation. Then slice the loaf and enjoy!

SNACK MEAL {CUCUMBER SANDWICHES}

2 cucumbers, peeled and thinly sliced
Dash of salt
2 T. white vinegar
Unsalted butter
2 T. cream cheese (or tzatziki—a seasoned yogurt-and-cucumber Greek spread)
4 slices favorite soft bread

Prepare the cucumbers, add a dash of salt and the vinegar, and let set for 30 to 60 minutes. Drain and set aside. Spread some butter and cream cheese (or the tzatziki) on each slice of bread. Make sandwiches, layering the cucumber slices. Cut away the crust and slice each sandwich into four triangles to serve.

4

LIGHT
AND
HOPE

Light

The natural agent that makes things visible by illuminating.

Hope

Grounds for believing that something good may happen.

We can rejoice, too, when we run into problems and trials,
for we know that they help us develop endurance.
And endurance develops strength of character,
and character strengthens our confident hope of salvation.
And this hope will not lead to disappointment.

ROMANS 5:3-5 NLT

When Jesus spoke again to the people, he said,
"I am the light of the world.
Whoever follows me will never walk in darkness,
but will have the light of life."

John 8:12

It was a crisp, cool autumn morning, and my family needed a break from the repetition, stresses, and flow of the everyday. We had been cooped up in the house for a few days, with me tending to projects and homeschooling the kids, and each of the kids diligently working to complete their schoolwork. Together, we decided we needed a breath of fresh air (literally) and embarked on a gentle hike through the mountains not far from our home.

In tow behind me were my four children, varying in ages from five to sixteen, and our beloved golden retriever, Penny. We marveled at the wonder of God's handiwork as we rambled deeper and deeper into the mountains, listening to the wind as it rustled through the aspen leaves and over the mountain pines. We gazed up at enormous boulders, standing all around us like giants from *The Lord of the Rings*. We took in sprawling mountain fields filled with prancing deer, soaring hawks, and hurried squirrels.

As we drank in the beauty around us, walking steadily along the winding, intertwining paths and through the stirring trees, we lost track of time—until suddenly, we noticed the sky growing darker. Then we paused to assess our location. We realized that after taking multiple turns, we were now lost deep in the forest.

My oldest began to worry, her brow furrowed as she glanced around with uncertainty. My youngest was growing tired, her little legs having far less stamina than ours. Try as we might to figure out where we were, to retrace our steps, to recognize which tree we had seen at which point, we simply could not get our bearings. The breathtaking nature we had been enjoying an hour earlier quickly turned into a landscape of anxiety-inducing unknowns. Every tree shadow was a possible hiding place for a creature, every echo was a potential looming threat, and every moment that passed was a chance for less and less hope to give way to more and more fear. Stories of mountain lions, bears, and coyotes filled our imaginations. With the night swiftly approaching, I went into mama bear mode. *What are my options?*

We had a cell phone, but there was no service that deep into the woods. The only option we had left was to press on and hope that somehow our trail would bring us back to the paths we knew, back to the safety of civilization. Hours later, we were still walking and searching for the way home. I felt a tightness spread across my chest, a worry festering in my mind, and a fear growing in the pit of my stomach. But with my children's eyes fixed on me, looking to me as their guide, I made the decision to bravely continue forward into the unknown. I felt both hope and fear wrestling for the spotlight in my mind as we continued on the barely visible path in front of us.

Finally, we sat down on some rocks to rest, drinking the last drops of our bottled water, and finishing off the last nibbles of our trail mix. I could tell my children were afraid, but I knew I had to rely on the last bit of hope I could muster. Quietly, under my shallowed breath, I prayed a short, desperate prayer to God to give us wisdom, hope, and light—to help us through this night.

Moments later, the sound of a roaring motor sliced through the stillness, serving as the soundtrack of deliverance. There was a light dancing through the trees, buzzing as it whipped around. We jumped off the rocks and started yelling, waving our arms. The light shifted toward us and glided in our direction. It drew closer and closer until finally a teenager on a dirt bike pulled up, as if he were a knight on a horse, and greeted us with a smile—he was the first person we had seen in hours, and it took every bit of self-control to not jump up and hug him.

With wide eyes he asked what we were doing in the forest at night. When we told him we were lost, those eyes brightened. He was excited at the thought of being the hero and rescuing a family from potential demise in the Rocky Mountains. He told us to stay put and he would return. Then he headed into the darkness. The next 15 minutes felt like days, but the valiant teenager made good on his promise. A while later, his tiny car pulled up, and the five of us, along with our golden retriever, piled into it. He drove us out of the wilderness and back to the warmth and safety that waited for us at home.

When it seems there is no way out of the shadows that envelop us, let's remember that God promises He is not only waiting on the other side of dark times, but also is walking through the darkness with us, holding our hands, guiding us, and acting as our source of light and hope.

Let's immerse ourselves in God's Word and conversation about light and hope.

God promises He is
not only waiting on
the other side of
dark times, but also
is walking through
the darkness with us,
holding our hands,
guiding us, acting as our
source of light and hope.

STEEP IN
SCRIPTURE TOGETHER

Through the story of Hannah, Scripture paints a picture of what it looks like to search for God's light in the midst of seemingly endless darkness, and to pursue hope even in our desperate moments.

Hannah was the wife of Elkanah. For many years, she was tormented because she remained childless, as she wholeheartedly wished for a child and found herself the subject of ridicule by others who did not empathize with her pain. Her anguish was so potent that she cried out to God:

Once after a sacrificial meal at Shiloh, Hannah got up and went to pray. Eli the priest was sitting at his customary place beside the entrance of the Tabernacle. Hannah was in deep anguish, crying bitterly as she prayed to the LORD. And she made this vow: "O LORD of Heaven's Armies, if you will look upon my sorrow and answer my prayer and give me a son, then I will give him back to you. He will be yours for his entire lifetime, and as a sign that he has been dedicated to the LORD, his hair will never be cut."

1 Samuel 1:9-11 NLT

Hannah's reliance on God's light through her darkest time led her out of despair, and she was eventually given a son: "In due time she gave birth to a son. She named him Samuel, for she said, 'I asked the LORD for him'" (1 Samuel 1:20 NLT). Hannah took this blessing seriously and raised her son to love and worship God:

After sacrificing the bull, they brought the boy to Eli. "Sir, do you remember me?" Hannah asked. "I am the very woman who stood here several years ago praying to the LORD. I asked the LORD to give me this boy, and he has granted my request. Now I am giving him to the LORD, and he will belong to the LORD his whole life." And they worshiped the LORD there.

1 Samuel 1:25-28 NLT

Our greatest weapon against the darkness of this world is God's light. We must cultivate eyes to see it and hope to pursue it, even when it feels as though the darkness will swallow us whole. Even though they may be hidden among the shadows initially, blessings are there in the dark times because we learn to rely on God's guidance. We trust in His promises with a fierce hope. And we discover His faithfulness in ways we can't when all is fine and we're strolling along under sunny skies.

When the sky is dimming and we cannot see a way forward, God is right there reaching for our hands. When we turn a new corner and worry about the unknowns, risks, challenges, or the faith God will require of us, God is still right there. He is eager to turn our trust in Him into blessings. Like Hannah, we can honor the blessings from God by surrendering them back for His purposes and plans. His light brings us hope. In turn, our hope in Him allows His purpose to shine from within us…preparing us to be a light to others.

Write your answers below and then take a moment to share them with one another.

When have you, like Hannah, received a moment of light and hope
from the Lord when you needed it most?

MOTHER

_____

_____

_____

_____

_____

_____

_____

_____

DAUGHTER

_____

_____

_____

_____

_____

_____

_____

_____

If in doubt MAKE tea

PASSAGES TO PONDER

There is so much light in Scripture that the Word of God is even called a light! Every step of the way, no matter what you face, there is insight, wisdom, truth, and hope in the pages of your Bible that will carry you, guide you, and show you the way. These are some favorite verses of mine to turn to when I need that next bit of light to see the way forward in God's will.

You are the light of the world. A town built on a hill cannot be hidden. Neither do people light a lamp and put it under a bowl. Instead they put it on its stand, and it gives light to everyone in the house. In the same way, let your light shine before others, that they may see your good deeds and glorify your Father in heaven.
Matthew 5:14-16

1. What does it mean to you to be a light before others?
2. Can you think of someone who is a light in your life?

Your word is a lamp for my feet, a light on my path.
Psalm 119:105

1. How has the Word of God acted as a source of light in your life?
2. What specific hope from God's Word has helped you recently?

The people living in darkness have seen a great light; on those living in the land of the shadow of death a light has dawned.
Matthew 4:16

1. Have you lived in darkness before, or have you witnessed someone living in darkness?
2. Can you think of a time when you saw "a great light" in the midst of darkness?

POUR INTO YOUR GIRL'S HEART

Dear _____,

The God of light is with you. He is your hope every day, no matter what you are facing. When you face times of darkness, call upon His name to shed light on what you need to see, know, or hear to honor the path He has cleared for you. How fortunate I am to witness His light already leading your heart and steps. These are ways I am seeing His hope and light in your life lately . . .

_____

_____

_____

Today, I pour His hope into you as I read these verses personalized with your name.

Blessed is _____, who trusts in the LORD, whose confidence is in him. She will be like a tree planted by the water that sends out its roots by the stream. It does not fear when heat comes; its leaves are always green. It has no worries in a year of drought and never fails to bear fruit.
Based on Jeremiah 17:7-10

_____ will never walk in darkness, but will have the light of life.
Based on John 8:12

May your unfailing love be with _____, LORD, even as she puts her hope in you.
Based on Psalm 33:22

MOTHER'S PRAYER

Light of the world,

Thank You for guiding me and my daughter

through our stories and our paths of life.

I believe You will bring help and hope to _____ when times

become dark or her sense of possibility dims.

You are always faithful, and You are present to her.

Help me release my worries for the unknowns in my daughter's life

so that I am an example of leaning into Your promises.

You have been my hope and strength throughout my days,

and now I am thankful I can share about those times with confidence.

This is a reminder how even our hardest, scariest moments

can and will be turned into lessons in faith and blessings of hope.

In Jesus's name, amen.

DAUGHTER'S PRAYER

Light of the world,

I am grateful to learn more about the hope You give to Your children.

When I face hard days, struggle with friends,

or worry about my future, I know to look for Your light.

You will cast out the darkness of fear and fill my heart with light

so I won't lose hope.

You will shed light on my next step and reach for my hand

so I won't lose my way.

Jesus, You know the worries I carry right now.

Today, I hand them to You and anticipate with faith

the ways You will transform my story into one of light and hope.

In Jesus's name, amen.

TWO FOR TEA

Where there's tea there's hope.

SIR ARTHUR PINERO

Whether you are beginning or continuing a tea tradition, you're building a legacy of discipleship and connection. This bit of respite in a busy day reminds our hearts how light and hope truly are within our grasp daily. In this moment, you're able to find rest and inspiration because you have first tasted encouragement during your intimate and ordinary times with the Lord. Just see how much hope is communicated during the simple act of sharing a pot of tea. It's a wonder!

❖

A SIMPLE POT OF TEA

Pour fresh water into your kettle and put it on the stove to boil. Choose whichever kind of tea you would like. Sometimes I use a couple bags of Yorkshire Gold and add an extra bag of Earl Grey.

Add a tea bag for each person, plus one, in the pot. Pour the boiling water into the teapot. Also pour a bit of the hot water in each teacup and swirl it around to warm it, and then toss that water. This ensures that the cups will become warm and keep the tea hotter longer.

Like these sweet times together, the tea is best when it isn't rushed and is allowed to steep a few minutes. If you would like to take your tea in the English tradition, make it a strong brew with milk—not cream—and some sugar to taste.

Make It Special

When you pause to take a sip of tea, be thankful for the shared silence. You and your daughter will delight in the sweetness of experiencing God's presence in the conversation and the stillness.

❖—❖❖❖—❖

Let light be your centerpiece. My favorite choice is a pretty candle or a pair of candles with flowers in the center. You can also illuminate your time together by draping twinkle lights along a curtain rod or your fireplace mantel. Or fold a battery-powered strand into a jar and place that as the centerpiece. Write the verse from John 8:12 on a blank card and set it next to the candle or jar.

❖—❖❖❖—❖

Have some uplifting music playing in the background. Perhaps some praise music or a playlist of happy tunes you and your daughter enjoy. Keep the volume low so conversation is easy but high enough that the inspiration can feed your spirits in moments of silence.

❖—❖❖❖—❖

Hope and light offer powerful imagery to deepen your daughter's connection to these faith characteristics. Have sketch paper and colored pens on the table so you both can draw one thing that represents the light of the world and one thing that represents hope.

❖—❖❖❖—❖

As an alternative activity, write out the first stanza of Emily Dickinson's famous poem, "'Hope' Is the Thing with Feathers" and place it on the table. You both can draw an image inspired by it. Next, choose a favorite verse about hope to handwrite beneath the drawings.

TEATIME TREATS

Light and hope bring to mind thoughts of caramel, brown sugar, and buttery goodness. There is no dessert more perfectly suited for today's tea than a warm, golden, rich, delicious butterscotch bar.

THE PERFECT BUTTERSCOTCH BARS

2 cups brown sugar
⅓ cup unsalted butter (softened)
2 large eggs
2 tsp. vanilla extract
2 cups all-purpose flour
¼ tsp. salt
1½ tsp. baking powder
1 cup butterscotch chips

Preheat the oven to 350° F. In a large bowl, beat the sugar and butter until smooth. Add in the eggs and vanilla and beat until creamy. In a separate bowl, whisk together the flour, salt, and baking powder. Gradually add the dry ingredients to the egg mixture, beating at a medium-low speed until just blended. Fold in half of the butterscotch chips.

Pour the batter into a greased 9 x 13-inch baking pan, spreading evenly. Sprinkle the rest of the butterscotch chips evenly across the top. Bake for 28 to 33 minutes or until an inserted toothpick comes out clean. Allow to cool for a few minutes.

Cut into squares while the bars are still warm and enjoy!

These sandwiches have a subtle sweetness that will go nicely with your tasty dessert. The croissants add a touch of elegance for your teatime.

2 cups baked chicken or supermarket rotisserie chicken, chopped
½ cup mayonnaise
(or a tad bit more if you feel the mixture needs to be more moist)
½ to 1 cup vanilla yogurt, to taste
½ cup salted buttered pecans or slightly roasted pecans, chopped
½ to ¾ cup seedless red grapes, chopped
Salt and pepper to taste
3 to 4 croissants

Mix the chicken, mayonnaise, and yogurt together, and then fold in the chopped pecans. Add the grapes last so they aren't over stirred. Add salt and pepper to taste.

Slice the croissants in half horizontally. Add a light touch of mayo to each side of a sliced croissant before loading up with chicken salad. Cut the sandwiches in half for easier eating.

Serve with chips if desired.

5

FAITH
AND
FAITHFULNESS

Faith

The quality of being true to one's word or commitments,
as to what one has pledged to do, remaining loyal and steadfast.
Acting on what you believe is true about God in your life.

Faithfulness

Adherence to something to which one is bound by a pledge or duty.

Let love and faithfulness never leave you;
bind them around your neck,
write them on the tablet of your heart.
Then you will win favor and a good name
in the sight of God and man.

PROVERBS 3:3-4

Without faith it is impossible to please God,
because anyone who comes to him must believe that he exists
and that he rewards those who earnestly seek him.

Hebrews 11:6

As young, hopeful, and idealistic parents of four, my husband and I had big dreams—dreams of changing the world, of making a difference, of leaving our mark...our wallet, however, didn't always concur.

We always knew we wanted to dedicate our lives to ministry and to help bring others to Christ, but life so often seemed to conspire against those dreams we believed God had placed on our hearts. Never more so than when, with three kids under 12 and another on the way, we were squeezed out of a church we had helped grow by pouring so much of ourselves into it. We were out of money and options and had to move in with my husband's mother, all the way out in a tiny sort of ghost town called Walnut Springs, Texas, where we would more likely encounter snakes than people.

When we initially said "I do" a little over a decade earlier and cast our vision for the future with our young, optimistic hearts, this was not what we had in mind. Things were not lining up with the long-held hopes and desires we had lengthy, late-night conversations and long-winded prayers about for years. By our time line, we should have been leading a large, robust ministry, impacting people's lives across the globe, and bringing them closer to their creator. Instead, we were in the middle of nowhere, with messy children, living with my mother-in-law!

I began to feel deep despair, wondering if God had forgotten about us or if we had gotten our dreams wrong. It was then that we realized we had a significant choice to make. We could allow hopelessness to fester in our hearts, or we could make the choice to trust God even in the middle of this literal desert.

Day after day, I put on a brave smile for the kids, trying my hardest to give them the best childhood I could. After putting them to bed each night, I would sit on the back deck, breathe in a few moments of peace, and gaze into the magnificent Texas sky. It was there, in the quiet and stillness of twilight, I would ask God if He remembered me, if I mattered, and if any of my hard work and the deep desires that continued to live in my heart meant anything at all.

Each day, even when I did not feel like it, I made the choice to get out of bed, thank God for small blessings, and offer up my hope for the future into His loving hands. I decided to be faithful with where I was and with what I had, even though most of it did not align with the life we had envisioned.

And so, with every new day, I would craft tasty meals, educate the children, provide them with adventures, and read books to them; at night, after talking to God for a while, I would write the words of what would eventually become my first book.

My husband, in lockstep with me, bought a desk and placed it in an abandoned old house on the property and began the long, tedious, unending work of conceptualizing and putting together a ministry, with no guarantee of success.

Looking back, now more than 30 years down the line, I wish I could tell my younger self just how important, formative, and significant those days were. How every sigh and prayer *did* matter, how every decision to smile for my children and work on my book, even when I had no assurance that anyone would ever read it, would lead to the life I have been blessed enough to live today—one of many books and a ministry that takes us around the world.

I could not see it then, but the difficult choices I made—even while in the dark, to walk in the direction of the Lord and what I felt He had put on my heart through the steady and often unseen acts of faithfulness—all mattered. Not only will these choices matter in this life, but they will also echo into eternity, affecting my children's lives and so many others down the line.

We cannot see God face-to-face in this lifetime. But when we live our lives in the truth of His reality, it not only pleases Him, but it also shows the world the reality *of* Him through the ways we live. When we exercise our faith and choose to be faithful at every age, it pleases Him for us to believe in His reality and presence.

Let's immerse ourselves in God's Word and conversation about faith and faithfulness.

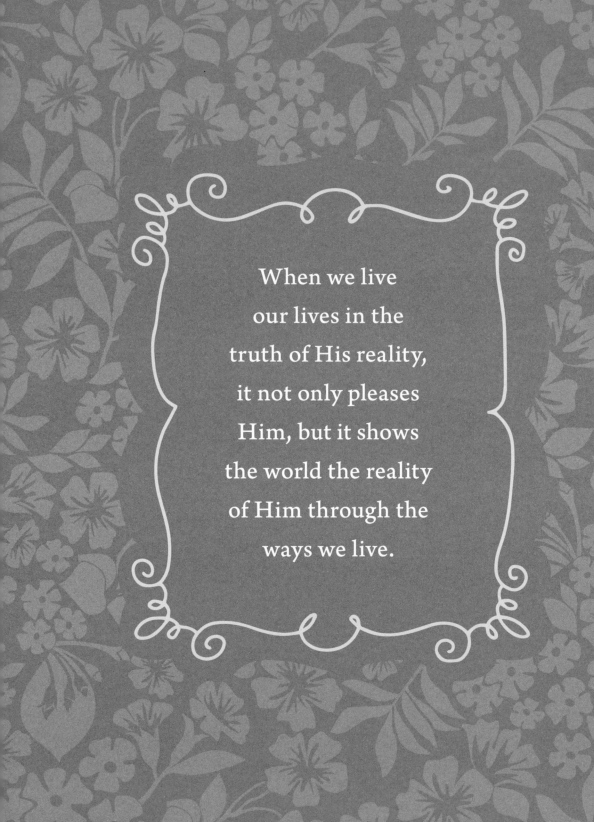

When we live
our lives in the
truth of His reality,
it not only pleases
Him, but it shows
the world the reality
of Him through the
ways we live.

STEEP IN SCRIPTURE TOGETHER

Faithfulness is a quality that is deeply important to God, and one of my favorite examples of this powerful trait is offered to us through the story of Ruth and Naomi.

Ruth was one of Naomi's daughters-in-law. After Naomi's two sons passed away, she was left with only her mourning daughters-in-law. Naomi told Ruth and Orpah, her other daughter-in-law, to go back to their own mother's homes and find new husbands. While Orpah decided to follow Naomi's instructions, Ruth chose to stay by Naomi's side:

Ruth replied, "Don't urge me to leave you or to turn back from you.
Where you go I will go, and where you stay I will stay. Your people will be my
people and your God my God. Where you die I will die, and there
I will be buried. May the LORD deal with me, be it ever so severely,
if even death separates you and me." When Naomi realized that Ruth
was determined to go with her, she stopped urging her.

Ruth 1:16-18

So Ruth began working in a field to pick up leftover grains. The field belonged to a man named Boaz, who recognized Ruth's loyalty, devotion, and faithfulness to Naomi even in a time of great despair:

Boaz replied, "I've been told all about what you have done for your mother-in-law since the death of your husband—how you left your father and mother and your homeland and came to live with a people you did not know before. May the LORD repay you for what you have done. May you be richly rewarded by the LORD, the God of Israel, under whose wings you have come to take refuge.

Ruth 2:11-12

Ruth eventually married Boaz and had a son—who was part of Jesus's ancestral line. When she was grieving the loss of the life she planned on and faced a decision she never expected to make, she had no guarantees. Yet the unknowns, fears, and doubts didn't prevent her from stepping forward in faith to follow Naomi. Her continued acts of faithfulness, big and small, led to her being blessed by the Lord. We can imagine that Ruth also wondered if God had forgotten about her, especially after losing her first husband, but He never abandoned her.

During our lives, we'll experience many moments, challenges, choices, and transitions that provide opportunities for us to demonstrate our faithfulness to God. Those are also the times we witness God's faithfulness to us. When we walk forward in faith and honor Him, there will be situations when our expectations for the outcome don't line up with what is unfolding. We might have days or seasons when we look around and wonder if we heard Him right or whether we took a wrong turn or were left behind along the way. This is when our faithfulness to God is all the sweeter. It requires a wholehearted surrender to His hope for us. As difficult as that may be when we're tired or disappointed or even scared, the fruit of following God wherever He leads—just as Ruth followed Naomi—is living the story He has planned for us.

Write your answers below and then take a moment to share them with one another.

Have you ever felt forgotten by God? How have you, like Ruth, remained faithful when waiting?

MOTHER

_____

_____

_____

_____

_____

_____

_____

_____

DAUGHTER

_____

_____

_____

_____

_____

_____

_____

_____

If in doubt MAKE tea

PASSAGES TO PONDER

The world can complicate the meaning of faith. But as a child of God who longs to grow in faith, you can have a clear understanding of what it means to trust God and follow His ways. You can move forward with belief in His sovereignty and the story He has set in motion through you. In these verses, may you find the comfort and clarity I have found over the years.

Faith is confidence in what we hope for and assurance about what we do not see.
Hebrews 11:1

1. Do you find it difficult to believe in a God you cannot see?
2. What assurance do you have about who God is?

Trust in the LORD with all your heart and lean not on your own understanding; in all your ways submit to him, and he will make your paths straight.
Proverbs 3:5-6

1. When has leaning on your own understanding led you in the wrong direction?
2. Can you think of a time when you felt God making "your paths straight"?

Let us hold unswervingly to the hope we profess, for he who promised is faithful.
Hebrews 10:23

1. When have you struggled the most to trust in God?
2. Do you believe that God is faithful to us?

POUR INTO YOUR GIRL'S HEART

Dear _____,

When you trust God early in life, your story will be rich with examples of what it looks and feels like to be faithful in all circumstances. What a gift this is as you grow older and can recall how God has been with you through good times and hard times. And when you share your faith with a friend, you'll have so many examples of His love in action. I'm grateful to see your faith and faithfulness in these ways...

_____

_____

_____

Today, I pour into your heart words of faith as I read from these personalized verses:

Truly I tell you, if _____ has faith as small as a mustard seed,

she can say to this mountain, "Move from here to there,"

and it will move. Nothing will be impossible for her.

Based on Matthew 17:20

We remember before our God and Father _____'s

work produced by faith, her labor prompted by love,

and her endurance inspired by hope in our Lord Jesus Christ.

Based on 1 Thessalonians 1:3

Consider it pure joy, _____,

whenever you face trials of many kinds,

because you know that the testing of your faith

produces perseverance. Let perseverance finish its work

so that you may be mature and complete, not lacking anything.

Based on James 1:2-4

MOTHER'S PRAYER

Faithful Shepherd,

I'm thankful for the goodness of faith in my life and the ways

You are building faith in _____'s life. May our time of fellowship

and connection help her see Your hand in our day-to-day experience

as we also explore putting our faith in You for our futures.

Fill _____'s heart with Your truth and love so her first response

is to trust Your leading. When she faces a challenge or a

time of sadness, may it become an opportunity

for her faithfulness to grow, take root, and bear fruit.

Today, I ask You to fill _____ with a longing to know

You, to trust Your way, to live her story, and to give You glory.

In Jesus's name, amen.

DAUGHTER'S PRAYER

Faithful Shepherd,

I'm learning more about You every day!

As I spend more time in Your Word and talk

about the faithful people in the Bible,

my eyes are opened to the ways I can walk with faith too.

Jesus, show me how I can be faithful today with the little things,

so You will entrust me with the big things that will be a part of my story.

I place my faith in You because I know You will never leave me.

I trust You to hear my prayers even when I whisper them in my heart.

Thank You for my family and the legacy of faith they give me.

In Jesus's name, amen.

TWO FOR TEA

*"I can just imagine myself sitting down at the head of the table
and pouring out the tea," said Anne, shutting her eyes ecstatically.
"And asking Diana if she takes sugar! I know she doesn't but
of course I'll ask her just as if I didn't know."*

L.M. MONTGOMERY, *ANNE OF GREEN GABLES*

Spending intentional time together will nurture an appreciation of the gifts of listening, being heard, and being in fellowship. One-on-one exchanges, and even shared times of silence, warm us with their intimacy and comfort us in their safety. The teapot and the cups can be unremarkable at first glance. The tea can be ordinary and inexpensive. But when the steam rises and the splash of cream or sprinkle of sugar swirls, and you look at one another over the delicate rims, a plain day becomes extraordinary and meaningful.

FRUIT-INFUSED HOT TEA

4 cups boiling water	⅓ cup sugar
4 tea bags	¼ cup lemon juice
¼ tsp. ground cinnamon	¼ cup orange juice
¾ tsp. whole cloves	Orange or lemon slices

When your kettle whistles, pour the boiling water over the tea, cinnamon, and cloves. Let this mixture steep for five minutes and then strain out the cloves. Now, add in the sugar and fruit juices to the tea and heat this mixture to just before the boiling point. Serve hot with a lemon or orange slice in each teacup. This recipe makes 4 servings.

Make It Special

The more you meet for tea and discipleship, the more naturally it
will feel and flow. Make room for the conversation to bloom.

Select a cheery perennial flower to place in a single flower vase. Consider a sunny
Shasta daisy or a lush peony or a wine-red rose. Perennials represent faithfulness as
they return to grow and show their beauty year after year.

Before your teatime, draw a time line across a horizontal page, noting four to five of
the most significant times you experienced God's faithfulness in your life. Share this
with your daughter. Encourage her to make a time line too. It's very powerful to recall
God's faithfulness in our lives.

Create a memorable, tangible takeaway. At the craft store, buy colored beads,
lettered beads, and nylon string or thin satin strands. Read aloud Proverbs 3:3-4
and then set aside time during the tea to make personal necklaces so the
words "love" and/or "faithfulness" can literally grace your necks.

Play a praise song that incorporates Scripture. When it comes to the verse, pause
together to listen to it and take it in. Share this verse: "Faith comes from hearing the
message, and the message is heard through the word about Christ" (Romans 10:17).
How does hearing truth through God's Word build your faith?

TEATIME TREATS

Sometimes delicious treats spark a feeling of home, belonging, and comfort. As a bread maker, I created these buttery cinnamon goodies whenever my family needed a special little something to accompany tea in our afternoon, because it is always available and a favorite. Whether Sunday afternoons or raining or snowy days, they were always a hit. I almost always had some homemade bread in my freezer, but this recipe works great with any bread of your choice.

CINNAMON TOAST TRIANGLES

1 tsp. ground cinnamon
6 tsp. granulated sugar
Slices of your favorite artisan bread, or homemade bread as we do.
Butter

I always keep a little shaker jar on my counter filled with a cinnamon and sugar mix. I almost always double the mixture so that I don't run out.

Choose your favorite loaf of artisan bread. Making delectable loaves of oat-honey-wholewheat bread from freshly ground flour has been a practice of mine since I was a young married woman living in Vienna, Austria. You can purchase your favorite loaf at the store or make your own bread and freeze it until you need it.

Slice the bread and cut off the crusts if you prefer. Next, toast the bread until crisp. Butter it generously when it pops up from the toaster. While the butter is still melted, generously sprinkle the cinnamon sugar on top.

Gently shake off the excess sugar, leaving a crust of the sugar mixture on top. Cut the toast into four pieces, making triangles, and place onto a serving plate. You can also cut them into rectangles or logs and call them cinnamon toast fingers. As adults, our family prefers the toast in one piece, and we each often eat at least a couple. My husband, Clay, came up with the cinnamon mixture, and from the time our children were little, we have "feasted on" cinnamon toast.

This treat is best made as the tea is brewing. Tea and toast is a very British tradition, always served with a lot of butter and when the tea is almost boiling hot. If you do not serve the toast right away, wrap it in foil and keep it in the oven on low heat to keep the slices warm. If you prefer to have plain toast and butter, as we occasionally do, consider serving with raspberry jam as I do in Oxford, or strawberry as my husband prefers. Enjoy!

SNACK MEAL {FRUIT SALAD}

A simple fruit salad is a light and lovely offering to go with cinnamon toast.

Chopped apples
Chopped pears
Chopped dates
Cranberries
Sliced seedless grapes
1 T. lemon juice
5 T. mayonnaise
Chopped pecans
Cinnamon to taste

In a bowl, add all the washed and prepped fruit. Drizzle with the lemon juice and stir. Then add the mayonnaise to coat the fruit. Sprinkle with the chopped pecans and cinnamon.

6

STRENGTH AND STEADFASTNESS

Strength

The capacity of an object or substance to withstand great force or pressure.

Steadfastness

The quality of being resolutely or dutifully firm and unwavering.

Even young people tire and drop out,
young folk in their prime stumble and fall.
But those who wait upon GOD get fresh strength.
They spread their wings and soar like eagles,
They run and don't get tired,
they walk and don't lag behind.

ISAIAH 40:30-31 MSG

She is clothed with strength and dignity;
she can laugh at the days to come.

Proverbs 31:25

I watched through the car window as the flat, golden fields of West Texas zipped by. We were making our way down a long, empty stretch of highway with few stops except for the occasional shabby gas station, sometimes separated by 100 miles.

We had been in the car for 17 hours, the sweltering, relentless sun beating down on our old minivan filled with me, my husband, and our four children—ranging from a fussy four-year-old all the way up to an angsty fifteen-year-old.

Road trips are often romanticized in books and movies. More times than not they are described or depicted with wide open spaces, belly laughs, bonding between friends, carefully curated playlists, stops at quaint roadside cafes, and the making of memories. But our romantic visions of road trips don't revolve around four bored, frustrated, weary kids stuffed into a small space for hours on end. The novelty had worn off. This was our version. And this was long before the entertainment and distraction power of iPads and in-car screens. Toys and books were scattered across the seats, but they had lost their appeal about 300 miles earlier.

We were embarking on a new adventure with many more unknowns than knowns. I am the first to admit to experiencing the butterflies-in-the-stomach excitement that comes with not having all the answers and moving forward in spite of the question marks. When we have a heart conviction and are following God's lead, we're fueled by a different kind of energy and determination than when pursuing plans set in motion by humankind. The uncertainties don't matter because we're following the certainty of God's wisdom and promises. Encountering and overcoming obstacles with God's strength builds our resolve to see a journey through to the end.

However, there is a point in such a journey when old thoughts or new concerns can find their way into our minds. The catalyst for a moment of doubt might come after a friend or stranger asks a question that gives us pause. Or maybe a forced detour causes us to fear we got off the path God intended. In this moment, it is essential to keep our eyes on the goal set before us originally and to summon the strength to keep going.

During the physical journey my family was on, I hit that moment as we rolled through the seemingly never-ending sunny fields of Texas. The road trip felt much longer than I had anticipated, and our destination seemed elusive at best. I was road weary and not feeling the strength I did when we packed the car with a tank full of gas and hearts full of joyful determination. After what I would have sworn was a lifetime of driving through dusty deserts and open pastures, listening to bickering from the back seat, and diffusing implosions of impatience, something resembling a row of bumps appeared ahead of us, far in the distance. Gradually, they grew larger as our car crept along the deserted highway road.

Bubbling over with excitement, I whipped around to look at the kids, exclaiming, "Everyone, look!" There were mountains on the horizon. They were small—hardly visible—but unmistakable. We all *oohed* and *aahed* over this glorious, brand-new sight. Taking in the steep hills, gorgeous tree-filled valleys, and winding river bends were a beautiful and welcome contrast to the flat hills of Texas we had lived among for so long. As we got closer, I put my hand up against the window and felt the crisp air dancing just on the other side of it. I couldn't wait to breathe in the fresh mountain air and feel it in my lungs and across my face.

Just like that, with the sight of the gargantuan, blue Rocky Mountains looming ahead, all the hours of petty fusses, heavy sighs, and *Are we there yet?* inquiries seemed to drift away and vanish in the presence of the quickly approaching beauty. After 17 long hours on the road, we finally arrived at the bottom of the mountains and encountered a majestic landscape that made the difficult trip worthwhile.

Life is so often weighed down by chaos, taken over by uncertainty, and wrought with challenges. When we press on, when we're willing to embrace the unknown and follow with steadfastness the road God presents, we will be given the greatest gift: experiencing the beauty and grandeur of God.

Friend, when you don't give up, you will model for your daughter what strength of faith looks like. When you press on through the difficulties of life, the seasons of uncertainty, and the times of more questions than answers, you are strengthened and so is your example of leaning into God's strength. The eyes and ears of the young are paying attention…and so are their hearts.

Let's immerse ourselves in God's Word and talk about strength and steadfastness.

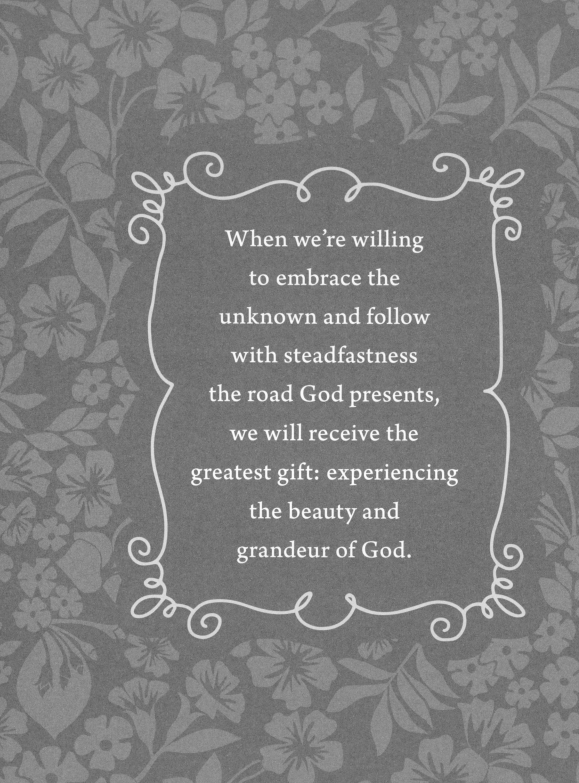

When we're willing
to embrace the
unknown and follow
with steadfastness
the road God presents,
we will receive the
greatest gift: experiencing
the beauty and
grandeur of God.

STEEP IN SCRIPTURE TOGETHER

Scripture offers us a wonderful image of what it looks like to hold fast to God's promises, to remain steadfast and strong in the face of difficulty through the story of Esther.

Esther was a young Jewish woman who, through her winsomeness, beauty, and intelligence, found favor with the king of Persia and became queen—all while keeping her Jewish identity a secret. But after learning of a plot to kill her people, Esther courageously resolved to save them:

Esther sent this reply to Mordecai: "Go, gather together all the Jews who are in Susa, and fast for me. Do not eat or drink for three days, night or day. I and my attendants will fast as you do. When this is done, I will go to the king, even though it is against the law. If I perish, I perish." So Mordecai went away and carried out all of Esther's instructions.

Esther 4:15-17

Esther was in a position of privilege and did not need to take a stand and speak up. She could have stayed silent and safe. Yet she risked it all and changed the fate of God's people. This Bible story of Esther as a heroine of strength and faith shows us how she used her charm, tenacity, and loyalty—her influence and cleverness—to convince the king to allow her people to defend themselves:

The king and Haman went to Queen Esther's banquet, and as they were drinking wine on the second day, the king again asked, "Queen Esther, what is your petition? It will be given you. What is your request? Even up to half the kingdom, it will be granted."

Then Queen Esther answered, "If I have found favor with you, Your Majesty, and if it pleases you, grant me my life—this is my petition. And spare my people—this is my request. For I and my people have been sold to be destroyed, killed and annihilated."

Esther 7:1-4

Esther's strength in the face of injustice, violence, and even possible death saved her people: "For the Jews it was a time of happiness and joy, gladness and honor. In every province and in every city to which the edict of the king came, there was joy and gladness among the Jews, with feasting and celebrating" (Esther 8:16-17). On one day, the Jews were at risk of annihilation, and on the next they are rejoicing—all because one woman intervened. She shed light on Haman's dark plan of destruction, and in turn the king had Haman killed rather than allowing the Jewish people to suffer. The dramatic change truly came down to one decision and one point of surrender. Esther went forward knowing she could fail; she could perish just for asking.

Being steadfast in our daily life comes down to being faithful even when we could fail, even when our friends or strangers might judge us, even when our point of surrender could upend everything we have known.

To experience the gifts of God's goodness, beauty, faithfulness, and generosity, we must remain strong and steadfast in the face of whatever storm, stress, and suffering comes our way.

Write your answers below and then take a moment to share them with one another.

In what areas of life are you leaning into God's strength more than usual? Are there areas in which you're struggling to press on with full faith?

MOTHER

_____

_____

_____

_____

_____

_____

_____

_____

_____

DAUGHTER

_____

_____

_____

_____

_____

_____

_____

_____

If in doubt MAKE tea

PASSAGES TO PONDER

Scripture is filled with encouragement and inspiration to stay strong and steadfast despite the hardship, pain, and adversity we encounter in life. Here are some of my favorite verses about strength that I return to in times of difficulty or doubt.

In this world you will have trouble. But take heart! I have overcome the world.

John 16:33

1.   What feelings rise when you realize you will encounter trouble in your life?
2.   Can you think of reasons in your own life to "take heart"?

The Lord is my strength and my song; he has given me victory. This is my God, and I will praise him—my father's God, and I will exalt him!

Exodus 15:2 NLT

1.   What does this verse mean when it says the Lord is "my song"?
2.   Can you think of ways in which God has given you victory?

Be strong and courageous; do not be afraid; do not be discouraged, for the Lord your God will be with you wherever you go.

Joshua 1:9

1.   Do you believe that God is with you wherever you go?
2.   When has God's presence comforted you?

POUR INTO YOUR GIRL'S HEART

Dear _____,

I'm grateful to have a front row seat to watch you become the young woman God created you to be. I see your personality, gifts, and interests unfolding in lovely ways. It isn't easy at your age—or any age—to wait on the Lord when you need answers or want to know how everything will turn out, but stay strong in your faith. The Lord won't leave you in one place when you desire to grow. Lately, I've witnessed your spiritual growth and strength in these ways:

_____

_____

_____

Today, I pour strength into you from God's Word with these personalized verses:

Do not fear, for I am with you, _____;

do not be dismayed, for I am your God;

I will strengthen you and help you;

I will uphold you with my righteous right hand.

Based on Isaiah 41:10

Those who hope in the LORD will renew their strength.

_____ will soar on wings like eagles;

_____ will run and not grow weary,

_____ will walk and not be faint.

BASED ON ISAIAH 40:31

My dear _____, be strong and immovable.

Always work enthusiastically for the Lord,

for you know that nothing you do for the Lord is ever useless.

Based on 1 Corinthians 15:58 NLT

MOTHER'S PRAYER

My Strength,

Fill _____ with strength that comes from Your heart and hand.

Give her faith in Your works and power so that when

she encounters difficulties,

she can stand strong in You. She can voice her faith with conviction.

She can move forward even if others might not agree or understand.

Grant _____ a heart in tune with Your own so she will know Your will

and the way You ask her to go. Jesus, give_____ a steadfast spirit

that leans into Your strength when she is weary or nervous.

In those moments of surrender, fill her with peace and understanding.

May she know she is doing Your will and honoring

You with every steadfast step of faith.

I can't wait to see the ways You will shape my

daughter's story for great things.

In Jesus's name, amen.

DAUGHTER'S PRAYER

My Strength,

Thank You, Jesus, for giving me strength to live my story. I trust I can

turn to You in every circumstance. You are with me wherever I go.

You give me a heart of courage when I'm afraid,

and You give me peace when troubles come.

Help me look to my mom and other women of faith—including those

of the Bible—to understand how You love and lead Your children.

Jesus, I'm ready to be steadfast in the godly ways

I care about others, serve You,

walk in faith, and stay encouraged. Even when

I cannot see what You have up ahead for me,

I will trust the next step. You are my strength, Lord. And my song.

I pray my story creates a melody that is pleasing to You.

In Jesus's name, amen.

TWO FOR TEA

"A woman is like a tea bag;
you never know how strong it is until it's in hot water."

ATTRIBUTED TO ELEANOR ROOSEVELT

The bond between moms and daughters is strengthened with each conversation about life, faith, and what matters most. Sharing from the heart is a practice that grows and becomes stronger the more often it happens. Each of these teas is an invitation to invest in this practice and build up one another in heart, mind, and spirit.

A woman of faith doesn't fully know her strength or that of God until she faces a difficult time and trusts His might and faithfulness. Then when she shares with another woman about those experiences, their hearts are emboldened, their faith emboldened. It's a beautiful legacy of strength.

EARL GREY TEA

Many people choose Earl Grey tea as a replacement for coffee. It's not just for breakfast, but if you are sensitive to caffeine, it may be wise to have earlier in the day.

To introduce this tea and make it an inviting blend for your daughter, serve it in a classic way with a slice of lemon and a bit of sugar to taste. Early Grey is made with black tea and has oil of bergamot, so the lemon complements the subtle citrus of this popular tea. Most drink it without milk unless the black tea base is particularly strong.

Make It Special

If you have time to prepare, consider what your daughter needs most. Could she use a pick-me-up? A celebration? Comfort? This discipleship time will feed her spirit.

◆━◆━◆

Plan a special invitation based on what your daughter needs. Roll up a small piece of paper with an invite on it and place inside a balloon (of her favorite color, of course) before you blow it up. Tie the inflated balloon to her room's doorknob or wherever she will see it. Another possibility: With a marker, write an invite on a rock and reference Psalm 18:2 ("The Lord is my rock").

◆━◆━◆

Years ago, I found a lovely antique pedestal dish at a secondhand store. It literally elevates the presentation of goodies while also elevating the table's beauty. It makes me think of God upholding us with His righteous right hand (Isaiah 41:10). Find a similar piece that represents to you the strength of God.

◆━◆━◆

On a piece of paper, write the letters S-T-R-O-N-G vertically. During your time, consider creating an acrostic by assigning a characteristic of faith to each letter. For example: Steadfast, Trustworthy, Redeemed, Openhearted, Noble, Growing. Or write a prayer using these letters to begin each line.

TEATIME TREATS

Everybody loves chocolate! When I think of strength and steadfastness in dessert form, a rich, classic, yummy chocolate cupcake is the first thing that comes to mind. To make this teatime extra special and memorable, try adding an extra dose of chocolate chips to these cupcakes and then top them off with a luscious, creamy chocolate buttercream frosting.

DOUBLE CHOCOLATE CHIP CUPCAKES WITH CHOCOLATE BUTTERCREAM FROSTING

Ingredients for the cupcakes
¾ cup flour
½ tsp. baking powder
½ tsp. baking soda
Pinch of salt
½ cup cocoa powder
2 eggs
⅓ cup vegetable oil
3½ tsp. vanilla extract
½ cup dark brown sugar
½ cup granulated sugar

½ cup whole milk
1 cup chocolate chips (I usually use semi-sweet, but any will do)

Ingredients for the frosting
6 T. unsalted butter (softened)
2 T. whole milk
½ cup cocoa powder
Pinch of salt
2½ tsp. vanilla extract
3½ cups powdered sugar

Preheat the oven to 350° F and line a 12-cup cupcake pan. In a large bowl, whisk together the flour, baking powder, baking soda, salt, and cocoa powder. Then, in a separate bowl, whisk together the eggs, oil, vanilla, brown sugar, and granulated sugar; once combined, slowly add to the dry ingredients, alternating between the egg mixture and the milk, until all ingredients are just combined. Fold in the chocolate chips, careful not to overmix.

Pour the batter into the liners (around halfway). Bake for 17 to 23 minutes or until a toothpick inserted into the middle of a cupcake comes out clean. While the cupcakes cool, make the frosting.

With a handheld or stand mixer, beat the butter until smooth (a minute or two). Then mix in the milk, cocoa powder, salt, and vanilla extract. Add in the powdered sugar slowly, working out all the clumps.

Once the cupcakes have cooled, top them off with the chocolate buttercream frosting. You will delight in these melt-in-your-mouth treats.

SNACK MEAL {FRUIT PLATE}

When serving a rich dessert that will be the focal point and object of anticipation,
a simple and colorful fruit plate provides just the right complement. Below are some
suggestions that will go nicely with a chocolaty dessert. For a pretty presentation,
choose at least three options. And, of course, feature fruit your daughter loves.

Bunches of seedless grapes
Sliced apples in a couple varieties
Sliced pears
Strawberries
Pomegranate seeds

Arrange the fruit nicely on a platter or on individual plates. If you serve pomegranate seeds, place them in a small crystal or glass bowl.

7

LOVE AND DEVOTION
{BIRTHDAY TEA}

Love

*Deep affection for another which leads to commitment
and generous expression.*

Devotion

*Love, loyalty, or enthusiasm for a person, activity, or cause:
religious worship or observance.*

*I am reminded of your sincere faith, which first lived in
your grandmother Lois and in your mother Eunice
and, I am persuaded, now lives in you also.
For this reason I remind you to fan into flame
the gift of God, which is in you through the laying on of my hands.
For the Spirit God gave us does not make us timid,
but gives us power, love and self-discipline.*

2 TIMOTHY 1:5-7

We love because he
first loved us.
1 John 4:19

Birthdays are a very special event in the life of our loved ones. These once-a-year days are about celebrating the person, leaving them feeling affirmed, loved, and excited about living a great story. *Their* great story. Birthdays are an invitation to create a day where deeper connections are forged, companionship is shared, and, at the end of the day, the special birthday person is filled with love to the point of overflowing. Our family goal is to always leave the birthday person with an overwhelming sense of being loved, affirmed, and encouraged in our intimate circle of life.

One of the sweetest illustrations of this kind of love is from my connection to grand-daughter Lilian. We don't live in the same town all year long, but when we do have time in each other's presence—even if it isn't her birthday or mine—we have this cozy and unconditional affection and appreciation for who the other is and for the relationship we've formed by being intentional to seek each other out.

Oxford, England, is my home about six months a year. I work in a church there to mentor graduate students and wives. I'm so fortunate to have three of my grandchildren living in Oxford too. I cherish every moment I get to spend with them. My oldest grandchild, Lilian, has become my constant companion whenever I can visit her home and spend the night there in their guest room. Of course, I love all my grandchildren but at four, Lilian can better communicate her thoughts. It is our custom that every morning when she awakens, she is allowed to wake me up. Sometimes we snuggle in bed together, and I tell her stories in which she is the heroine.

Other days, without waking up the others in the house, we slip quietly downstairs to the kitchen, where I make myself a strong cup of black tea in a china teacup. For Lilian, I choose a children's china mug I picked out for her. I drop about a tablespoon of tea into her cup, with one teaspoon of sugar or honey and fill the rest up with milk. This way, it looks slightly brown like mine but is mainly milk. She loves it, and we officially call it "Lilian's special tea." We then proceed to the living room, where she sits in a ratan children's size chair I bought her when she was two. (I got it for a deal at a local charity/secondhand store.) I sit in an overstuffed chair near her, and we chat as friends and sip our tea. It has become an expected ritual since she was two years old.

Sometimes I invite her into my squishy, comfortable chair with me. I tell her, "You are beloved and very special to God and to me. I like who you are. You are a great dancer to delightful music, you help me, and you are a kind friend and lots of fun to be with. I am so glad God let me be your grandmother."

One day she asked to climb into my lap. She squished up tightly against me and cuddled her head under my chin.

"You know what I was thinking, Queenie?" she asked, using my grandchildren's name for me. "When you cuddle me and sing songs to me and tell me stories, it makes me feel really good inside. I am glad we are friends."

This brought happy tears to my eyes and filled my heart with grateful joy. She chose to express the most important value to me. To know she loves to be in my presence, that she longs to be with me, and enjoys it whenever we are together is what I, as a grandmother, long for. Love is the emotional oxygen we crave in order to feel valued, to understand our worth, and to be close in relationship to others. Love was extremely important to Jesus. We all long to be loved, and when we act in loving ways to others, they will see God in our words, actions, and behavior.

I do not expect Lilian to be perfect or to do great deeds for me. I just want to be with her and share the love we have created together. In that way, this is God's love and grace I am pouring into her. And, honestly, I receive it right back from that little heart.

If you are celebrating your daughter's birthday or your daughter could use a day that reminds her of her precious value, fill her with this kind of love. The gift isn't in material presents but in the giving of time and devoted attention. And her treasure isn't found in party favors; it's in the discovery of being favored and beloved by God.

Let's immerse ourselves in God's Word and conversation about love and devotion.

We all long to be loved,
and when we act in
loving ways to others,
they will see God
in our words, actions,
and behavior.

STEEP IN SCRIPTURE TOGETHER

When I think of my sweet times with Lilian and the gift of such a connection, I'm reminded of Mary of Bethany and her love and devotion to Jesus. Mary was the younger sister of Martha, a very capable woman. Jesus loved them both and considered their home to be a place where He was welcomed. Throughout His ministry, He often went there to be with His friends (Mary, Martha, and their brother, Lazarus), and He would share a meal and rest in good conversation and their friendship with Him.

One evening, Jesus and some of His friends had come to their house. We can read about it in the book of Luke:

As Jesus and the disciples continued on their way to Jerusalem, they came to a certain village where a woman named Martha welcomed him into her home. Her sister, Mary, sat at the Lord's feet, listening to what he taught. But Martha was distracted by the big dinner she was preparing. She came to Jesus and said, "Lord, doesn't it seem unfair to you that my sister just sits here while I do all the work? Tell her to come and help me."

Luke 10:38-40 NLT

Martha, the older sister, had a good heart. But her head was focused on the big dinner she was planning for Jesus and all His friends. Certainly, we can relate to wanting everything just right for a special guest. But her stress was leading her away from the important thing that Mary understood.

Mary was so excited that Jesus came to her home. She felt about Jesus like my sweet granddaughter Lilian felt about me—she just wanted to be with Him, to be close to Him, to cherish her friendship with Him and His love. And you know what? That's what Jesus wanted the most—her love and close relationship.

Jesus spoke gently to her. "My dear Martha, you are worried and upset over all these details! There is only one thing worth being concerned about. Mary has discovered it, and it will not be taken away from her" (Luke 10:41-42 NLT).

God wants our love, our companionship, our desire to sit with Him. Loving one another, developing a close relationship, and speaking encouraging words of love are important things to God, and Mary showed us what they look like. Even as Lilian wanted to be with me and told me in her own words, so God loves it when we, His children, delight to be with Him and tell Him so. This is the root of real worship—an authentic love for our God expressed through our affection and devotion for Him.

You see, we are God's treasure, the art of His creative hand, and shaped to live a unique story in Him. He crafted you with your personality, dreams, and circumstances as a place in which you're able to live a vibrant life and able to flourish and bring His reality to bear. He sees you and cares for you every day.

God calls us His beloved (Colossians 3:12 ESV), which means we are precious to Him and most dearly loved. When we model this love to our daughter, especially in honor of her birthday, we are reminding her of the legacy of which she is a part. And we can encourage her to embrace the boldness and love God bestows on her so she can serve at His feet and do so as her unique self.

Write your answers below and then take a moment to share them with one another.

When have you been like Martha—preoccupied with details?

When have you been more like Mary—eager to sit at the feet of Jesus?

MOTHER

_____

_____

_____

_____

_____

_____

_____

_____

_____

DAUGHTER

_____

_____

_____

_____

_____

_____

_____

_____

If in doubt MAKE tea

PASSAGES TO PONDER

God's Word reveals the many ways He loves us and cares about every part of our lives. He formed us and marvels at His creation. He wants nothing more than to be in relationship with each of us…His beloved children. I hope you draw closer to Him through these verses.

> You made all the delicate, inner parts of my body and knit me together in my mother's womb. Thank you for making me so wonderfully complex! Your workmanship is marvelous—how well I know it.
> **Psalm 139:13-14** NLT

1. God crafted your personality, your whole self, and pronounced you "marvelous"—how does this make you feel about yourself?
2. What do you like most about the way God made you?

> I am saying this for your own good, not to restrict you, but that you may live in a right way in undivided devotion to the Lord.
> **1 Corinthians 7:35**

1. How does responding to God's love give you freedom instead of limits?
2. What is one of the ways you've showed devotion to God lately?

> Whoever loves God is known by God.
> **1 Corinthians 8:3**

1. When did you first love God?
2. What does it mean to you right now in your life to be known by God?

POUR INTO YOUR GIRL'S HEART

Dear _____,

You are God's beloved. I see the gift of who you are in the world, in my life, and in the lives of others. Spending time with you is priceless. Whether we're quiet together or talking about school, your friends, your faith, or your dreams, it is treasured time. I am blessed by knowing you and seeing your heart. Here are a just a few reasons why I love you and admire the way you love...

_____

_____

_____

   During this special time together, I want to pour love and grace into that great heart of yours as I read these personalized verses. May you take them in as proof of how beloved you are.

Dear _____, let us continue to love one another,
for love comes from God. Anyone who loves
is a child of God and knows God.
Based on 1 John 4:7 NLT

I am convinced that nothing can ever separate _____ from God's love.
Neither death nor life, neither angels nor demons,
neither her fears for today nor her worries about tomorrow—
not even the powers of hell can separate _____ from God's love.
No power in the sky above or in the earth below—indeed, nothing in all creation will
ever be able to separate _____ from the love of God
that is revealed in Christ Jesus our Lord.
Based on Romans 8:38-39 NLT

MOTHER'S PRAYER

God of Love,

Every day I am grateful for the birth of _____, and

today I am thankful to celebrate it with this time together.

My heart for her reminds me of Your heart for me, her, and all Your children.

With great tenderness and joy today,

I thank You for _____'s growing love for You as Lord

and for Your care and provision for her.

I'm blessed to witness to the unique story You are unfolding through her.

There will be surprises, challenges, and many joys,

and You will be beside her for every one. This I can count on.

Through it all, I pray _____ will respond to Your

great love with service, devotion, and a passion to

share that love with others every day and year of her life.

In Jesus's name, amen.

DAUGHTER'S PRAYER

God of Love,

Thank You for giving me life.

As I learn more about Your character and about the character

You are growing in my heart, I realize how much You care

about every decision and step I make and my every hope and prayer.

Before I understood Your love, I experienced it through my mom.

I pray You will continue to draw us closer to one another and to You.

Give me courage to express my devotion to You when with friends,

family, and those You place along my path.

Thank You for my life...and for the bigger story

You have for me as Your daughter.

In Jesus's name, amen.

TWO FOR TEA

Enjoy life sip by sip, not gulp by gulp.

THE MINISTER OF LEAVES

Taking tea together is a way to slow down and pay attention not only to our lives, but also to the story of the one sitting with us. It's so easy to go about our days hurrying from this errand to that task, gulping down food, and talking over one another. By shifting your attention to one another, you're hitting the pause button and choosing what really matters.

As Mary sat at the feet of Jesus, may we do the same with Him and then with devotion to one another. Each time we do, we say to one another, "You matter. Your story matters. Our relationship matters." What better time than a birthday to savor memories and moments you take in sip by sip with gratitude.

JAM TEA

Brew a pot of English Breakfast tea
Provide an assortment of jams, such as strawberry, cherry, or raspberry
Sugar to taste
Whipped cream for extra fun

Select a jam that will delight your daughter. Add 1 teaspoon jam in the bottom of each teacup and then pour the hot tea. Add sugar and perhaps a bit of whipped cream for a festive display and tasty treat.

Make It Special

A birthday is the perfect time to create a unique cup of tea for your daughter just as Lilian and I did. Together, think through the flavors your daughter loves, which of the teas you've tried so far, and what the perfect tea recipe for her might be. Then, of course, name it after her! This will be a special connection between you for years to come.

❖━━◆◗▮◖◆━━❖

Who says you can't put a pretty birthday candle on a scone?
Make it fun with a sparkler candle or one that is your daughter's favorite color.
Sprinkle a little confetti or curled ribbon on the table.
Anchor a shiny helium balloon in her favorite shade to her chair.

❖━━◆◗▮◖◆━━❖

In *The Sound of Music,* character Maria cheerfully sings about how having tea with jam and bread is one of her favorite things. Let that inspire this sweet time celebrating the day your daughter's story began by filling it with her favorite things. What does she love when it comes to flavors, music, activities, and topics? Have her create a fun list and then chat about it.

❖━━◆◗▮◖◆━━❖

A special gift will be just the thing. Perhaps a new teacup if your daughter hasn't selected one before. Other gift categories well suited to these discipleship moments would be: a monogrammed Bible, a pretty journal, or a bookmark or decor piece featuring your daughter's favorite verse. Keep it simple and set it apart from any other birthday gifts. Save it for this teatime together.

TEATIME TREATS

A traditional tea with scones will be a grown-up touch as you celebrate your growing girl. Not only are these scones delicious, but also they can be made with a flavor she loves. Whether you use jam made from berries you picked together or a regional favorite the two of you chose at a local outdoor market, these will be memorable and unique—just like your girl.

JAM SCONES

2½ cups flour	2 eggs
3 tsp. baking powder	Jams of choice
2 tsp. sugar	(Choose a flavor that will com-
½ tsp. salt	plement your jam tea selection.
¼ cup butter	Cherry, raspberry, and orange
5 T. milk	marmalade are lovely options.)

Preheat the oven to 450° F. Sift together the flour, baking powder, sugar, and salt. Cut in the butter until you have a coarse consistency. Stir in the milk with a fork. Separate one egg and slightly beat the white, setting aside one tablespoon of it to use for the glaze. Add the remaining egg white and yolk with the second egg and beat together. With a fork, stir into the coarse flour mixture.

On a floured board, roll out the mixture to a ¼-inch thickness. Cut into squares (2½ to 3 inches). Select your jam of choice and place 1½ teaspoons of jam in the center of each square. Fold opposite corners to the center and pinch together.

Place the scones on greased cookie sheets and brush lightly with the tablespoon of egg white. Sprinkle with a little sugar and then bake for 15 minutes. Serve warm with a bit of quick clotted cream.

QUICK CLOTTED CREAM

In Oxford, clotted cream is in abundance! A delicious dollop is placed on scones for a touch of sweetness. In America, however, clotted cream isn't as common. However, this creation is a fine substitute to enhance your teatime treat. Try it and then compare it to the real thing next time you travel across the pond.

1 (8 oz.) carton whipping cream
2 to 3 tsp. granulated sugar
½ tsp. vanilla extract

Whip the whipping cream and sugar together in a bowl until soft peaks form and then add a capful of vanilla extract. Simple, sweet, and a lovely complement to scones and other baked goods.

SNACK MEAL {CHARCUTERIE BOARD}

While "charcuterie" means cold meats, these days a charcuterie appetizer board is more like a personal buffet. Curate your selections of meats, cheeses, nuts, and fruit based on what your birthday girl loves. Sprinkle in variety to have a pretty and colorful array of treats. If you don't have a charcuterie or cutting board, use a platter or large plate, or find something else in your home to serve as a fun surface, such as a pretty, framed 18 x 24 mirror or a round one for a unique touch.

Roasted and salted walnuts or
pecans or Marcona almonds
Clusters of purple grapes
Sliced salami and/or other proteins
Sliced cheeses (your daughter's favorite)
Wedge of brie

Boursin cheese to spread
Crackers
Cherry tomatoes
Popcorn
Rich chocolate truffles or squares

Nibble to your heart's content.

8

HUMILITY AND OBEDIENCE
{CHRISTMAS TEA}

Humility

On the ground, lowly, to bend, kneel, or bow before the presence of someone.
Obedience and submission to one greater.

Obedience

Compliance with an order, request, or law or submission to another's authority.

Have this mind among yourselves, which is yours in Christ Jesus,
who, though he was in the form of God, did not count equality
with God a thing to be grasped, but emptied himself,
by taking the form of a servant, being born in the likeness of men.
And being found in human form, he humbled himself
by becoming obedient to the point of death, even death on a cross.

PHILIPPIANS 2:5-8 ESV

Then the man—Adam—named his wife Eve,
because she would be the mother of all who live.

Genesis 3:20 NLT

I just love Christmas! Don't you? The sparkling lights, delicious cookies, and glorious music that highlights one of the world's most historically important events—the birth of God coming into the world to save it! But, as I have read the Christmas story many times and imagined what took place, I am amazed at the fact that most of the people who played an important part were normal people living mundane lives. I think God loves using people like you and me to tell His story in the world. I'll share with you what I mean.

Lines of women formed in front of my book table, which was piled high with my newest works. Timid in demeanor, one sweet woman walked up and almost whispered her question as I was signing her books.

"Sally, I want to write a book, but I have three children under the age of five. I wonder if you could tell me what I need to do to become a published author and how to control my children so that I can find time to write."

My answer did not please or excite this sweet one. I think she wanted an easy answer, and much of life is about living a steady and good story, growing little by little and working over a long period at the ideals we cherish inside. I said:

Be faithful to give your whole heart and energy to loving your children well
in this season, to practice growing in patience, obedience, and gratefulness.
Put your energy into the story you have been given right now. Whatever free

time you can find—even 10 to15 minutes at a time—be sure to study the Bible, practice praying to God, read great books, and write down what you are learning in a journal. Then you will store up wisdom that comes from living a life of integrity, so that when your schedule naturally opens up, you will write wisdom that was gleaned in the quiet, hidden, faithful moments of your life. That is usually where deep, wise inspiration is formed.

Everyone's story and capacity are different. But if it is truly something you were made to do, you will eventually find a way. Just don't sacrifice your priorities along the way because that is where your authenticity lies.

When I look back on my own life, birthing four children, having three miscarriages, moving 20 times (multiple times internationally), and living through the seasons of their growing up years, I realize that most of my life was spent loving my family well in the midst of chores, character training, thousands of meals, and lots of cleaning up our messes over and over again while seeking to grow spiritually and intellectually along the way. I was hidden in the rich soil of shaping a great life.

I had promised to be faithful to Jesus, and I believed He had directed me to give my whole self to passing on a legacy of faith, training in character, living joyfully and intentionally, and caring for my family's needs. Most of the giving of my life in worship of Him was invisible to the outside world. I did not get an award for washing one more dish, lifting up one more prayer for a child's decisions, or kissing one more forehead after a bad dream. Or getting up at 4:30 a.m. to write what I was learning in my journal. Yet I always had the desire to please God and be obedient to what He had for me to do, so that kept me going through the hidden years. What we do when no one is looking shows the integrity of our lives. To live by our convictions even when no one else notices becomes the most important work of all because that choice honors God and not ourselves. What we practice, we become.

Living the humble existence of a praying, teaching, guiding, and loving parent might not result in awards, but, believe me, there are many *rewards*. You will bear rich fruit in your life as you embody the story and purpose God has spoken into being for you. And you will witness the fruit in your child's life again and again as they grow into their story. Your words speak life over your child, and your nurturing care and biblical discipleship give life to them as well. Don't ever worry that you are not where you think you should be. Don't give power to doubts about not living up to your potential. When you are obedient to God, trust Him, and humbly walk with Him step by step, you are right where you need to be...and you are who you need to be—a receiver and a giver of life.

Let's immerse ourselves in God's Word and talk of humility and obedience.

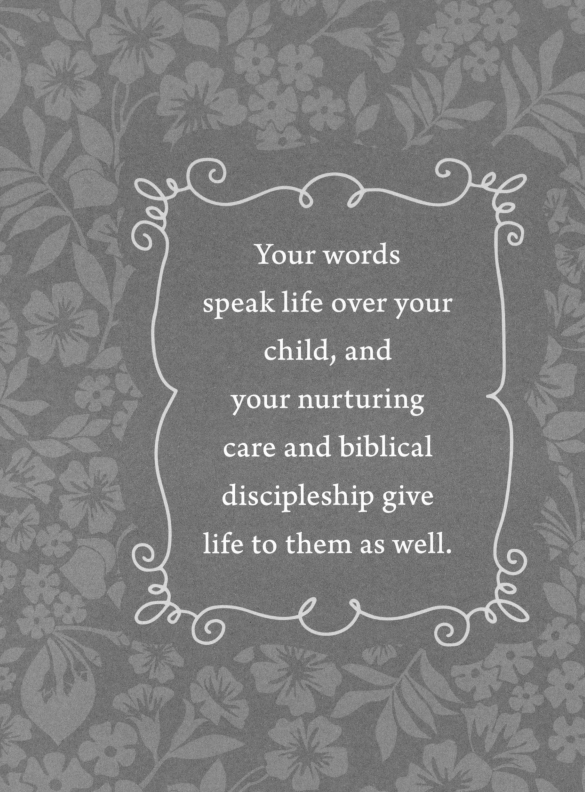

Your words
speak life over your
child, and
your nurturing
care and biblical
discipleship give
life to them as well.

STEEP IN SCRIPTURE TOGETHER

Mary, the mother of Jesus, is one of my favorite women in Scripture. She shaped history in profound ways by carrying and birthing Jesus, the Savior of the whole world, through her own body. Nursing Him through sleepless nights, rocking Him to sleep, teaching Him to walk, reading the Bible to Him daily and training Him as a child was what formed most of her life. Most of her works of faith were hidden from the world of great people and accomplishments, yet her life of birthing God into the world was one of the greatest works anyone ever committed to.

I've often wondered how God picked Mary to be the mother of Jesus. And yet we have some clues that show us why God chose her:

In the sixth month of Elizabeth's pregnancy, God sent the angel
Gabriel to Nazareth, a village in Galilee, to a virgin named Mary.
She was engaged to be married to a man named Joseph,
a descendant of King David. Gabriel appeared to her and said,
"Greetings, favored woman! The Lord is with you!"

Luke 1:26-28 NLT

This angel announced to Mary that God was with her, favored her—in other words, God delighted in Mary. He loved her in a special way. I wonder if God had seen a special heart of humility in Mary through the years. Perhaps she was faithful to worship Him, to practice being obedient to Him, to being faithful in small things, so He knew she would be a worthy mother to Jesus?

When the angel appears to Mary to tell her she would bear the Son of God into the world—bring Him to life through her own body—"Mary responded, 'I am the Lord's servant. May everything you have said about me come true'" (Luke 1:38 NLT).

Mary would be a faithful, generous, and loving mother to Christ because she considered herself a servant of God in everything she did. Her self-image was that her life was about following and being obedient to God every day.

To serve God and do what He asks with such faithfulness and a spirit of surrender requires great humility. Mary was willing to bow her knee, to give honor and obedience to God in anything He required of her. And He was requiring a lot of this young woman. How did she say yes so willingly? She was frightened, and yet she also had a righteous fear of the Lord. Her faith was so beautiful that she was even able to pray that all God's plans would come to fruition. She didn't rattle off a list of conditions first; instead, she said yes, stepped forward in her calling, and never looked back.

That heart of humility and obedience was the instrument through which God's life, through Christ, entered the whole world and delivered His salvation and love. When we give ourselves to God as a servant, we can also become the vessel through which He brings His life, salvation, and beauty into the world. We birth His reality, His life-giving grace every day as we choose to love, choose to live within and give from the common and mundane places of our lives. This is what it looks like to bear God's life to our world, our community, our family, our daughter.

Write your answers below and then take a moment to share them with one another.

What is so powerful about Mary's humility? What do you sense God is asking you to say "Yes!" to in your life?

MOTHER

_____

_____

_____

_____

_____

_____

_____

_____

_____

_____

DAUGHTER

_____

_____

_____

_____

_____

_____

_____

_____

PASSAGES
TO PONDER

Again and again we are reminded of the gifts we experience as God's chosen, His adopted children, and His faithful followers. In all these roles we are called to be humble and gracious as new creations in Jesus. I share these verses so you'll remember the blessing to walk in faith and in your story and your new life in Christ.

As God's chosen people, holy and dearly loved, clothe yourselves with compassion, kindness, humility, gentleness and patience.
Colossians 3:12

1. What might it look like to "wear" humility and kindness?
2. Which of the attributes in this verse are hardest for you to live out? Why?

This is love: that we walk in obedience to his commands. As you have heard from the beginning, his command is that you walk in love.
2 John 1:6

1. How have you been obedient to walk in love lately?
2. What is hardest about honoring God's command to walk in love?

Always be humble and gentle. Be patient with each other, making allowance for each other's faults because of your love.
Ephesians 4: 2 NLT

1. What specific ways can you practice patience with your family and friends?
2. Who has been a living example of humility and gentleness? How about patience and forgiveness?

POUR INTO YOUR GIRL'S HEART

Dear _____,

Mary devoted her life to please God. This prepared her to be the mother of Jesus. When you are willing to be His servant, God uses your life right where you are. He will use you to bring life, beauty, goodness, and love to your world. As we celebrate Christmas, think about how you can be like Mary. Ask God to help you to be humble and obedient in your chapter of God's story. As your mom, I'm blessed to see these ways that you humbly honor life as God's daughter...

_____

_____

_____

Today, may I encourage your spirit of humility and obedience as I read these verses personalized with your name.

Take my yoke upon you, _____,
and learn from me, for I am gentle and humble in heart,
and you, _____, will find rest for your soul.
Based on Matthew 11:29

Everyone has heard about your obedience, _____,
so I rejoice because of you; but I want you to be wise about what is good,
and innocent about what is evil.
Based on Romans 16:19

He died for _____ so that she who receives
his new life will no longer live for herself.
Instead, she will live for Christ, who died and was raised for her.
Based on 2 Corinthians 5: 15 NLT

MOTHER'S PRAYER

Jesus—Son of Mary,

I count my blessings, and there are many.

When we celebrate Your birth, I am humbled that

You include me and _____ in Your ongoing story.

I have great affection for Your mother, Mary.

She was the first to show us how to love You.

These special times talking with _____

about You is one way we share in that love.

Thank You, Jesus, for loving my daughter as I do—

with unconditional love. You hold her close, and

You faithfully hear her prayers with great affection.

These treasured times together in Your presence are shaping

our hearts and our minds forever. Together may we

proclaim the good news of Your birth, life, and resurrection.

In Jesus's name, amen.

DAUGHTER'S PRAYER

Jesus—Son of Mary,

Thank You for being born into the world.

Your birth showed us what true humility looks like.

And Your mother, Mary, shows us what surrender and love look like.

Show me the way to go, Lord. Help me to live, speak, and serve

with humility and grace as I stay open to Your will.

I trust that You make all things new…including my

attitude, my hope, and my heart.

Thank You for my eternal life in You, Jesus.

Because You were born, I am blessed with a story of faith and purpose.

As Your humble and grateful daughter, may I use my life to give You glory.

In Jesus's name, amen.

TWO FOR TEA

[Tea-masters] have given emphasis to our natural love of simplicity,
and shown us the beauty of humility.

OKAKURA KAKUZŌ

I have always been fond of Christmas. As a young girl, all my senses took in the season's pleasures: twinkling lights, the scent of cinnamon and cloves, the glow of a decorated Christmas tree early in the morning, the taste of sugared pecans and gingerbread. And yes…the cup of tea warming my hands as I savored its comfort and the wintry view beyond my cozy seat by the window.

Christmas traditions take many forms. They are as unique as the individuals, families, communities, and churches that create them. I invite you and your daughter to make your discipleship teatime part of your traditions. You'll be so glad you did.

◆━━━◆❙◆━━━◆

CHAI TEA

Blend the scents and flavors of the season with tea and what do you have? A delicious cup of chai.
If you want to keep it simple, use a bagged chai tea and mix in a bit more Christmas cheer.

Brew 3 bags of chai tea in 3 cups of water
Pour into a saucepan, and over medium heat stir in:
⅔ cup milk
A pinch or two of allspice
½ tsp. honey

When mixture is nicely blended and heated, pour servings into each cup and add a cinnamon stick to each for a fun Christmas cuppa.

Make It Special

Add sparkle, wisdom, and beauty to your Christmas teatime. Reflect on the joy and new life you have received by having shared in these teatimes together.

Fill small crystal bowls with roasted buttered pecans. Stack dark chocolates wrapped in silver foil in a pyramid. Drape tinsel on the chairs for a regal, shimmery touch. Float the bloom of a chrysanthemum or poinsettia in a glass bowl.

Bring these teatimes full circle with a nod to the 12 days of Christmas. With a metallic pen, write the faith characteristics on a piece of black or red ribbon: Purpose, Confidence, Light, Hope, Faith, Faithfulness, Strength, Steadfastness, Love, Devotion, Humility, Obedience. Discuss how the gifts your True Love gives to your heart are changing your life.

Place a star-shaped decoration or ornament as the centerpiece.
Read Matthew 2:1-12 together and talk about how the Magi humbly followed the star to meet the Christ child. Then discuss how you both have followed God's light to draw closer to the Christ child.

Consider painting some premade ornaments from the craft store.
Or if you go shopping together in advance, you can each select an ornament to give to the other. Perhaps one with a special word or verse on it that represents this new teatime tradition.

TEATIME TREATS

A trifle is one of my favorite company deserts. Especially festive and quite special to eat, it is a light, layered, and beautiful offering. I make mine in custard or mini-parfait dishes, but you can also use juice glasses. I have some festive red juice glasses that make it a fun Christmas treat.

MINI TRIFLES

Pound cake, angel food cake, or lady fingers, chopped in small cubes or pieces
Favorite berries—strawberries, blueberries, blackberries, raspberries, fresh cherries

Whipped cream
Instant vanilla pudding mix or homemade vanilla custard

Order these items in an assembly line to make it easier to place them into each parfait cup, small juice glass, or small mason jar. First, put one layer of cake cubes into the bottom of the glass. Lightly cover the cake in pudding or custard. Next, layer one berry layer at a time so they show well on the outside of the dish for a pretty pattern. (For example: a blueberry layer followed by sliced strawberries, full raspberries, and then chopped cherries. Use 2 to 4 layers of fruit.) Next, spread another thin layer of the pudding or custard with small bits of the cake.

Finally, create a swirl of whipped cream and top with chocolate sprinkles, slivered almonds, light crystal sugar, or simply a single berry! Keep these refrigerated until you serve them. They can be made hours ahead of time.

SNACK MEAL {PINWHEEL SANDWICHES}

These little sandwiches are easy to make and light enough for mid-afternoon, and they create a lovely presentation when placed on a special platter. For a festive look, arrange them in a circle, like a wreath, on your plate.

3 10- or 12-inch flour tortillas
Cream cheese
Chopped chives
Chopped spinach
Chopped cherry tomatoes

On one side of a tortilla, spread cream cheese and then sprinkle chives, spinach, and finely chopped tomatoes to cover the circle. Roll tightly. Cut off the uneven ends and then slice to create multiple pinwheels. Place on a pretty plate. Personalize these with any added ingredients your daughter loves.

TIP: For more color or to match the green and red hues of the season, look for packaged tortillas made with spinach or tomato.

I pray you will keep meeting with your daughter for special times of mentoring and discipling. Whether you continue with teas or choose different intentional mentor opportunities as you go for walks or sit on the sofa and catch up on what God is doing in your life, your daughter will benefit from your attention as you tend to her heart and spirit with interest, care, and passion.

One of the simplest ways to keep your bond of discipling strong and to build your daughter's character is to stay in God's Word.

Whatever is true, whatever is noble, whatever is right, whatever is pure, whatever is lovely, whatever is admirable—if anything is excellent or praiseworthy—think about such things.

Philippians 4:8

Christ will make his home in your hearts as you trust in him. Your roots will grow down into God's love and keep you strong.

Ephesians 3:17 NLT

About the Author

Sally Clarkson is a bestselling author, world-renowned speaker, and beloved mentor who has dedicated her life to supporting and inspiring countless women to live into the story God has for them to tell.

Sally hosts a weekly podcast, *At Home with Sally*, where she invites you into her home, thoughts, and life to share her candid wisdom and winsome discipleship. She has authored more than 20 books, including *The Lifegiving Home, Educating the Whole-Hearted Child, Teatime Discipleship,* and *Different* (with her son Nathan).

Sally has been married to her husband, Clay, for 41 years, and together they founded and run Whole Heart Ministries, an international ministry seeking to support families in raising faithful, healthy, and loving children in an increasingly difficult culture. They have four children—Sarah, Joel, Nathan, and Joy—each exceeding in their own fields as academics, authors, actors, musicians, filmmakers, and speakers.

Sally lives between the mountains of Colorado and the rolling fields of England and can usually be found with a cup of tea in her hands.

With *Teatime Discipleship*, Sally will invite you in, pour you a cup of tea, and share with you what she's learned about how our incredible Lord reveals His glory through our home life, relationships, and daily responsibilities.

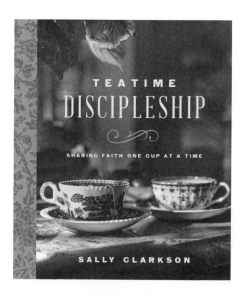

Cover by Faceout Studio, Amanda Hudson

Interior design by Faceout Studio, Paul Nielsen

Cover photo © Charnyshova Liudmila, Igor Norman, mama_Mia / Shutterstock

Definitions are from the Merriam-Webster Dictionary, https://www.merriam-webster.com.

Published in association with The Bindery Agency, www.TheBinderyAgency.com.

For bulk, special sales, or ministry purchases, please call 1-800-547-8979. Email: Customerservice@hhpbooks.com.

This logo is a federally registered trademark of the Hawkins Children's LLC. Harvest House Publishers, Inc., is the exclusive licensee of this trademark.

Teatime Discipleship for Mothers and Daughters
Copyright © 2023 by Sally Clarkson
Published by Harvest House Publishers
Eugene, Oregon 97408
www.harvesthousepublishers.com

ISBN 978-0-7369-8545-1 (Hardcover)
ISBN 9780-7369-8546-8 (eBook)

Printed in China

23 24 25 26 27 28 29 30 31 / RDS / 10 9 8 7 6 5 4 3 2 1